EVERYBODY WAS HAPPY

*The boy from Merritt Avenue,
the rise of Food Town,
and the myth of Marilyn Monroe*

HAP ROBERTS

Copyright © 2019 by Harold K. Roberts, Jr.
First Printing, November 2019
Third Printing, February 2022
Printed in the United States of America

All rights reserved. This book, or parts thereof, may not be reproduced, stored in a retrieval system, or transmitted in any form or by any means, electronic, mechanical, photocopying, recording or otherwise, without the written permission of the publisher.

Published by Roadhouse Books, LLC
Salisbury, North Carolina
Available In:

Hardback ISBN: 979-8-9851640-5-3
Paperback ISBN: 979-8-9851640-4-6
eBook ISBN: 979-8-9851640-3-9

Cover and book design by Sarah Michalec

Contents

Dedication..8

Acknowledgments....................................9

Preface...10

A word about my editor...............................12

College graduation, 1972..........................14

Part I: Growing up on North Merritt Avenue
    Early life..19
    My extended family....................................22
    Uncle Carl..24
    The cotton office..27
    The evils of liquor......................................28
    My friend Knee High.................................30
    The man in the rain...................................33
    Workers on the farm.................................35
    "He drove the car into the river"..............39
    The micro midget..40
    On to go-karts...41
    Around the cemetery................................42
    Trouble with the micro midget 42

The Big Game...44
Voodoo and Doo-Doo....................................47
Voodoo and the pool game...........................48
Ed Rufty's pool hall..49
The pond, the cave, and the copperhead....50
The $100,000 bills...52
The Soap Box Derby, lemonade stand, and
    Wachovia Bank...55
Families in the neighborhood.......................56
The talent show..60
My best friend for life....................................64
The neighborhood bully................................68
Fishing trip to Uncle John's farm.................69
Playing Army..72
Max Brockman...73
Daddy, the Highway Patrol,
    and the fishing trip..................................75
Cuba before Castro..80
First Presbyterian Church.............................81
High school memories...................................83
My own struggle..90
Concert list..95
Parking lot research.......................................97

Part II: The Food Town Years 1972-1982 and Beyond

Food Town..128
Buying mom and pop operations...............140
The Mavericks..145
Food Town quick takes...............................155

What did that nice man say to you?..........155
Crisco on sale for $1.98 at A&P...............155
Does your flounder come from
    High Rock Lake?.........................156
Don't approve checks from
    exotic dancers...............................157
A note about store numbers....................157
Ralph's first desk....................................158
Concrete-lined filing cabinets..................158
Dancing with Ruth Ketner......................159
Ralph Ketner's cuss jar...........................159
The stages of learning............................161
Doctrines from Mr. Ketner.....................162
Ralph Ketner's initial system..................164
A professional road map........................165
What if ?..166
All good things must come to an end.......167
Going into business for myself................168
Moving to Pine Tree Road......................169
Ryan's Steakhouses.................................170
Back in the groove..................................172
Origins of Statewide Title.......................174
A few words from longtime
    Statewide employees.....................177
The Statewide campus............................179
The dancer and the panic attack..............180
Mr. Ketner takes us to lunch...................181
Stewart Morris, Sr...................................182
The Heimlich maneuver..........................183
The Roadhouse.......................................184
Pack rat...186

My family..188
Annette Bell Roberts.................................192
"God had other plans"..............................193
The Cookie story.......................................194
Heather Roberts Brady..............................195
Sam's, cigarettes, and the credit card.......199
A therapeutic relationship........................200
Heather and the beach..............................202

Part III: Uncle Ralph and Marilyn Monroe
The uncle everybody wanted to have.......204
Preface to "Mimosa," an
    unfinished manuscript....................214
Marilyn's death...217
A bad day...218
Biography in Internet Movie
    Database (IMDb)...........................219
Various book acknowledgments...............220
Uncle Ralph and James Dean...................221
The Willa Cather connection....................221
Marilyn and Salisbury..............................222
The making of "The Misfits"....................223
"The Misfits," Mom and Me....................224
Norman Mailer...226
Architectural Digest.................................227
When Norma Jean turned into
    Marilyn Monroe.............................228
Flight insurance..229
The 50th anniversary of
    Marilyn's death..............................229

Elvis and Marilyn.......................................229
Marilyn Monroe's funeral........................230
The never-ending question:
    Hap's answer....................................231

Part IV: Our final thoughts
Life with Hap...234
Epilogue...236

Dedication

For my wife, Annette.
When we saw each other, it was truly love at first sight.
She continues to be the love of my life, my strength, and my rock — and she still "checks all the boxes."

For my daughter, Heather.
I have loved watching you grow into the sweet and beautiful lady you are today.

In loving memory of Idell McNeill Roberts and Harold K. Roberts, Sr., who supported me all through life and loved me unconditionally.

In honor of L.P. Bell, Jr. and memory of Joyce Barker Bell, my late mother-in-law, who encouraged me to start writing this book years ago.

In loving memory of Ralph L. Roberts, the uncle everybody wanted to have.

Acknowledgments

This book did not happen by itself. Many thanks go to a number of folks not listed in the preceding pages.

Thanks to Steve Jacobs, Jeanette Lassiter, Wanda Peffer, Chris Preslar, and the entire team at Statewide Title.

Thanks to my best friend Locke Long, Jr., along with Kee and Joyce Kirchin.

Thanks to Tom Smith and Sandy Lee for their contributions to the manuscript.

Thanks to our book and cover designer, Sarah Michalec.

Thanks to our early readers: Elizabeth Cook, Barry Hill, Dida Parrott, Cora Shinn, Mike Wenig, and Mark Wineka.

Thanks to Mark Wineka for the use of excerpts from "Lion's Share," used by permission.

Thanks to Ralph W. Ketner who did so much for so many.

And thanks to you for reading this book!

Preface

As I've often said, when someone dies, a library burns to the ground. The same thing happens when a man or woman gets dementia.

Dementia comes in on my mother's side of the family. Don't get me wrong. I hope I'm escaping all of it. I don't see any signs of it right now, and I don't want to see any signs of it, now or forever. But I've always hedged my bets. I've always tried to be a good pool player and think three or four shots ahead. That's why I said, OK, it's time, let's get started. Let's do a biography, and let's have input from others.

While I'm still sharp enough to talk and think, I want to write down my life story. While I've still got my faculties about me, I want to pour it all out. I want to give a few copies of this book to my friends and family, and I might want to print copies for some people who'd want to read it.

Probably 10 or 20 years ago, I started writing down a few notes. The best I could do was to jot down a few key words. I knew I could never sit down and write it or videotape it. I'm a people person, and I knew I had to connect with a person or persons, and have a connection where we hit it off and it would flow properly.

I'm a complex person, and this book is going to be complex. It's going to be something that appeals to people who are looking for humor, people who want to read about young boys growing into men and what they did afterward, people who want to know about overcoming adversity such as ulcerative colitis — how you can fight it and not let it get the best of you. If you can beat it, it can make you stronger. There will be something of interest to a college student who wants to be an entrepreneur, or to succeed in business, or to flow into a large corporation and hold a substantial position there.

This process has made me go back and soul search. Some things are humorous, some things are a bit painful, some things are a bit scary. Some of it's a lot of fun, some of it's not too much fun. Some you just want to keep in the back of your head. But I think it's a healthy process to bring it all out, warts and all, and say, "Well, overall, Happo, you've done a pretty good job, with yourself, your family, and your companies."

Most of all, it makes you realize how fortunate you are to have a God who looks after you, and surrounds you with guardian angels to guide you and protect you.

Hap Roberts
November 2019

A word about my editor

I love stories. I've been telling stories for years — the stories of my childhood, the stories of my time at Food Town Stores, Inc., the stories of my time as an entrepreneur with my own CPA firm and later, Statewide Title, Inc.

As I said in the preface, I've wanted to share these stories for a long time. There was only one problem. I had no idea how to do it.

I met Susan Shinn Turner at Ralph Ketner's funeral in June 2016. She introduced herself to me as she was covering the event for our local newspaper, The Salisbury Post. She had been on staff at the paper for nine years, and has been a freelance writer since 2013.

She was so prepared and so articulate. I was impressed. When I decided it was time to get serious about this memoir, I remembered Susan, and I felt like we'd have a good rapport and good working relationship. And we have.

Of course, it didn't hurt that she was a beautiful blonde who loved mimosas, just like another beautiful blonde you'll read about in this book. (To tell you the truth, she actually wrote that sentence, but I told her we could leave it in.)

Susan encouraged me to be as truthful as possible in the telling of these stories. We talked about the good, the bad, and the ugly. Some memories are funny, some are sad, some are downright painful. But I have tried to be as forthcoming as I can, and I truly hope you enjoy our efforts.

Susan is a native of China Grove, and a graduate of the University of North Carolina at Chapel Hill's School of Journalism. Her husband says it's her only flaw.

Susan's parents, Ed and Cora Shinn, live in Salisbury, and her son, Andrew Poe, graduated from Catawba College in 2019. Susan lives in Raleigh with her husband, Jim, but she traveled back and forth to Salisbury while we labored together on this project.

Susan is a good listener who makes others feel good about themselves. That is a gift. She is also an outstanding writer who improved each and every story I told her. That is also a gift. She told me that a favorite professor once advised her of her writing, "Make it sing."

Many thanks, Susan, for making my stories sing.

Hap Roberts
August 2019

College Graduation, 1972

As luck would have it, I forgot to tell my parents about my graduation from Catawba College. They made plans that week to visit Uncle Bob and Aunt Nell in Clearwater, Fla.

Despondent at first that they'd miss my graduation, I began thinking of things to ease that pain. How about a graduation party in my parents' back yard and my adjoining apartment, complete with a barbecue and some coolers of beer? Sweet.

I could get my friends Locke and Kee — yep, those are their names — to help get food, beer, ice, and other things we'd need.

My cap and gown were in my closet in my apartment, ready to go the next morning. I could go to the ceremonies. We had a plan! Sweet. Long story short, great party — really great. The last folks left around 2 a.m. after we listened to "I'm Your Captain" by Grand Funk Railroad.

Next day, mid-morning, I munched on a cold cheeseburger out of the fridge. I stood at an open window and watched the rain, the cool, cool rain. I glanced at my cap and gown, still in the closet. I looked out the window at the rain again.

What the hell was I going to do with my life?

1972: Graduation party at Hap's.

Part I: Growing up on North Merritt Avenue

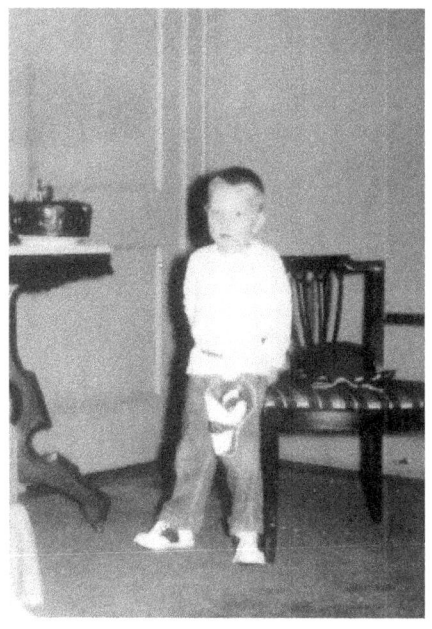

1954: A young Hap Roberts.

Early life

I was born Oct. 24, 1950, at Rowan Memorial Hospital here in Salisbury. My father knew all the doctors. He was a cotton broker with H.K. Roberts and Sons, along with my grandfather and uncle. They made a lot of money and lost a lot of money, but they made more than they lost, and that made a big impact in my life.

I was born at night — but not last night. As Bill Thompson once told me, I'm a complex individual.

My father was Harold Knox Roberts Sr., so I was named for him. So where did the Hap come from? I had an uncle, John Charles McNeill. Neat guy, they say. I never met him. The day after Pearl Harbor, he signed up for the Army. I think he had three deferments but he said, "What the hell," and signed up. He worked for the railroad.

His nickname was Hap. He was born a happy baby and called Happy John. Then it evolved into Happy and then Hap. He was a good dancer, liked the women, and had a gorgeous girlfriend he left behind. In his early 20s, he was on three landings during the worst battles of the Pacific. He was a machine gunner in the 27th Infantry Division, and had a crew of men that would take the machine gun off the boat and set it up.

The battle of Saipan was one of the most horrific battles of WWII. It was to be a joint effort between the 27th division and a Marine division. Several generals were involved and they got their signals crossed. They were waiting on the Marines, and Hap's group came under intense fire from the Japanese. Hap's men had to remove dead Japanese from his machine gun's line of fire. He used a 1917 Browning 30-caliber water-cooled Remington machine gun he had named "Little Sadie." The heat was so intense he had to rip his sleeves off and wrap them around the handles. On July 4, 1944, he went to the aid of a fellow soldier in his platoon who had been shot and was killed by a Japanese sniper. I had his medals released from the Pentagon in the 1970s.

My grandmother wanted me to be named after Uncle Hap. My father wanted me to be a junior. So I was named after him and nicknamed Hap. Everyone was happy.

My mother was Bonnie Idell McNeill Roberts. Her father and mother owned a general store in Richmond County near Rockingham. They also owned a feed mill and a farm. My grandfather McNeill was killed in the 1920s in an accident in his grain mill. My mother was 8, the fourth of five children. Hap was the youngest, and it was her duty to look after him. So when Hap was killed in WWII, she really had a double whammy.

My parents met in 1939 at N.C. State, where they went to summer school just that summer. They got married a year later. I'm an N.C. State fan by proxy. Daddy was taking some courses on cotton. Mama was going to be a teacher and was taking classes there. I don't know how they ended up there at the same time or even how they met. I guess it was meant to be. She finished at Catawba College and taught 20 years, mostly seventh grade, here in Rowan County. A great gal.

My grandfather was Hugh Kerr Roberts. He worked in the cotton mills from the time he was just a young boy, working his way up to superintendent of different divisions. The family moved around some as he was promoted. He retired from the mill when he was in his early 60s.

My grandmother, Lula Clementine Walker Roberts, died about that same time of cancer. Shortly thereafter, my granddaddy became a cotton broker, and my oldest uncle, Wilbur Franklin Roberts, was a partner with him. My dad left the Highway Patrol to join them in business.

My grandfather was not comfortable driving anymore, so Daddy did all the traveling. They set up offices on the third floor of the Wachovia Building, which are now offices for the City of Salisbury. That's where they began operations. After a year or so, they bought property at 1717 W.

Innes St., which was basically out in the country in the early '40s. They built an office with a small warehouse behind it, and continued to operate their cotton business.

My extended family

The boys in the Roberts family were drafted into World War II. Uncle Wilbur was too old to serve, and Daddy had high blood pressure and migraines. Uncle Clyde went into the Army Air Corps, and Uncle Ralph went into the U.S. Army, ending up as adjutant general in Burma under Gen. Joseph Stilwell. Before that, he was the first liaison officer between the newly opened Pentagon and the White House. Ralph, who was extremely smart, met with FDR on two different occassions. Uncle Dimp — Claude Murray Roberts — went into the U.S. Army, and fought in the South Pacific. He was my cousin Kent Roberts' father. He met my Uncle Hap briefly in Hawaii when they were going in two different directions. All the boys on the Roberts side of the family came back safely. Carl West Roberts had health issues that prevented him from working or serving. Uncle Brud — Walter Lee Roberts — worked for the Spencer Shops.

My aunts were Vera Roberts Eagle, Edna Roberts Myers, and Mabel Roberts Hoffner. They were great women, great mothers, great daughters to Papa, great cooks — true, God-fearing, Southern ladies.

Aunt Mabel's husband died when he was about 50. She went to Salisbury Business School, got her diploma, and went to work as a secretary at Rowan Memorial Hospital, working there until her retirement.

My maternal grandfather was John Alexander McNeill. He was industrious, an early entrepreneur. He owned a general store in Richmond County, down near Rockingham and Hamlet. He had a feed mill behind it, and he also had a farm. My grandmother, Ida Covington McNeill, kept the books. She could add up a row of figures in her head, so I guess that's where I get my accounting skills.

My grandfather was killed in a freak accident in the mill around 1923. He had the flu, but there was a problem with some of the machinery and he was mechanically inclined. They got him out of bed to come and check out the problem. He was wearing a long trench coat, which got caught in one of the gears. It pulled him down. He hit his head hard — and that was it.

Granddaddy was progressive. He had the first radio in Richmond County, and had ordered a biplane. Mama was 8 and Hap was probably 5 when he was killed. The biplane was never delivered.

Bob and Lura were the oldest children. Bob worked for the railroad. Lura went to business college and became corporate secretary of W.R. Bonsal and Co., a sand and gravel company for highway construction. They also invented Sakrete — a bag of cement to which you could add water. She had a good job. Aunt Lura's best friend was Ethlene Cochran, the sister of longtime N.C. Secretary of State Thad Eure. She was brilliant and cussed like a sailor. I just loved it. She'd say "damn" and "hell" and had a quick tongue. Mom and Aunt Lura would say, "Now Ethlene cusses a little. You don't need to repeat it."

Aunt Grace McNeill Pfeiffer was a secretary for the railroad, stationed in Richmond, Va. Her daughter is Sheila Pfeiffer King, and she is 10 years older than I am. She went to Pfeiffer and completed nurses' training at Emory University. She is married to Dr. O.W. "Fred" King, a vascular surgeon.

Uncle Carl

Uncle Carl was an alcoholic. He was a soft-spoken, neat guy — he just had that damn monkey on his back. He'd get drunk on Saturday nights, and my dad was always the one who had to go and bail him out. He lived in different apartments around town.

Occasionally, he got a job as a cook in a carnival. During Super Bowl IV in January 1970, I had my little apartment and Daddy came over and we were going to watch the Super Bowl. It was 16 degrees. Uncle Carl was down in Miami with the carnival on winter layover. Daddy just chuckled and said, "Here we are up here in 16-degree weather, cuddled up, and Carl is down there in 80-degree weather."

Daddy had a soft spot in his heart for Uncle Carl, and he sort of felt like he was his protector. When Daddy died, one of my other cousins took over that role. Not too long after that, Uncle Carl had to go to a nursing home. They let them smoke back then. Carl had his own chair in front of the television, and he'd sit there and smoke in the nursing home. He didn't drink in the nursing home, but his nerves were pretty well shot by then. He got to where he didn't want to go to family reunions anymore because of his nerves. He died in the 1990s from cancer.

When I worked at Food Town in the 1970s, New York bankers would come to visit as we expanded. I was really CFO, I just didn't have the title. The appointments with the New York bankers were made with me. They would all go downtown to the old T&F Barbecue on Council Street. It was sort of a rough part of town, but these bankers just loved to go down there, and I'd take them. I was assigned use, part-time, of a 1976 Pontiac Catalina. We'd pile in that car and I'd take them to T&F. One time, my stomach was bothering me. We had a lot going on and I wasn't on top of my game. I girded myself up and we went down to T&F Barbecue. There used to be an old grocery store down there on Council Street. Uncle Carl would go in there and buy wine. So I'm sitting at a stoplight waiting to turn left. My stomach is hurting. I look over and see Uncle Carl surrounded by five guys. He's telling a story and laughing. They're all having the time of their lives. Here I am with these high-powered bankers from New York. I said to myself, "What's wrong with this picture here? Something is not working out the way it's supposed to be."

Uncle Carl couldn't do a lot on the farm. He had something wrong with his leg, but Daddy would always have some task he would pay him for.

But Knee High, my dad's best friend, could do anything. One time, Knee High and I were in a corncrib shucking corn. We got down to the last of it and a mouse went up my leg. I hit it and it went on down. Then a mouse went up Knee High's leg. We decided it was time to quit.

Daddy had a huge pot there they'd make Brunswick stew in. Tom Atwell had a great recipe for Brunswick stew he'd make over a fire in that big pot. A couple of times, I'd get to go with Daddy and his buddies, and Knee High would stir it with a paddle. Mr. Atwell never wrote down the recipe. He got cancer and died, unfortunately. I talked to his daughters years later and they said, "No, Daddy never wrote anything down. He did it by memory."

That was the best Brunswick stew I ever had.

When they had nursing school at Rowan Memorial in 1950s, Daddy would always invite the students and his doctor buddies down for a cookout. They would have a big spread, and the student nurses would enjoy it.

The cotton office

I don't know how old I was when I went up to the cotton office. The first time I can remember I was 7 or 8 years old. But I was hooked. I loved the action. They had a ticker tape machine courtesy of Merrill Lynch, Pierce, Fenner & Beane — yes, Beane was part of the name back then.

When the secretary was at lunch, Papa would let me use the adding machine. I punched in one number after another and then when I had a tape taller than me, I stapled the tape and put it in a cigar box Dr. F. O. Glover had given me. I just loved it all.

Papa had two phones beside his desk — one local, one long distance. Both required operators. Once I sat in Papa's seat and picked up the long-distance phone. When the operator asked me the number I told her 3892, our home number. Then she asked me what city I was calling. About that time my Dad walked in and I hung up the phone. Whew!

Around 1960, it all came to a close. Papa died, and so did the cotton market. The mills started buying cotton in-house. Daddy had been financially conservative all his life. No Country Club. Just his farm and a great life his work had provided. We wanted for nothing. So what now?

The evils of liquor

My mother was raised a strict Southern Baptist. When her father was killed, she was taken to live with their minister, Dr. Ted Smith, for the summer. After that, she had an even stricter Baptist upbringing, spending the summer with the Smiths.

Alcohol was not part of her life. Now Uncle Hap drank. One fateful day, I was up at the cotton broker's office. I got tired of playing on the adding machine so I went back in the back office where they kept filing cabinets and cotton samples. I got tired of jumping off the rolled-up cotton samples and decided to peer into the filing cabinets — which was absolutely none of my business. I went into one, and lo and behold, there was fifth of liquor. I opened the next cabinet and there were two pints of liquor in there. Years later, I figured one belonged to Papa, one to Daddy, and one to Uncle Wilbur.

Being the liquor savior to the world, I took one bottle at a time out of the office. There were some woods next door with big rocks next to the cotton office. I set down a bottle, picked up a rock, and smashed it. First the fifth, then the two pints. Then I got to thinking, "What have I done?"

So I went back in, looking as innocent as possible, feigning a good time playing in the cotton room. Then 4:30 rolled around and everybody went back to the files, but no liquor was to be found anywhere. My heart was pounding. I figured it was time to go back and work on the adding machine. Daddy walked in and said, "Have you been messing in the filing cabinets?" I said, "No, sir." He said, "Are you sure you didn't get any bottles out of the filing cabinets?" I said, "No sir." There sat Papa with a disgusted look on his face, and Uncle Wilbur chewing on a half-smoked Lucky Strike. Daddy said, "Come with me."

As if he had radar, he walked over to the edge of the woods and peered in. Fortunately, Blackwelder's Barbecue was right across the street from the woods, and it was a teenage hangout.

They'd throw bottles across and break them on the rocks. As Daddy looked into the woods, my heart pounded. Surely I couldn't have a heart attack at 5 years old. Surely not.

Daddy left in his car and came back with a big bag, I guess to replenish the stolen loot. I was told to hone my skills on the adding machine and leave the filing to the secretary. I felt horrible.

That weekend, Mama and I went down to Hamlet to see my grandmother, "Mama Neill," and to visit with Aunt Lura. As we were driving down there, I told her, "Mama, I gotta tell you a story," and I relayed the story of the slaying of the three liquor bottles.

I said, "I'm so worried Daddy is gonna be mad at me."

I remember Mama reached over and hugged me and pulled me close and said, "Don't you worry, you probably did the right thing … But maybe you should never do that again."

I felt better.

My friend Knee High

My dad had a 550-acre farm on High Rock Lake he bought from The Aluminum Company of

America (Alcoa) for $6,433.50 on Feb. 22, 1946. He had a lot of water frontage, and he'd let me go down to the pier when I was 7 or 8 with Brownie, our Chesapeake Bay Retriever. I learned to swim at the Y so he didn't worry about me.

There was a black gentleman who was my dad's best friend. His real name was Robert Ferguson. His nickname was Knee High, but he was real tall. He and my dad were drafted at the same time, at the beginning of World War II, and Daddy drove them both down to Fort Bragg. They kept Knee High and sent Daddy home because he had migraines and high blood pressure. Knee High served in the black units in the Army that unloaded ships in the Pacific. He had a bad supervisor, a white man who did not like black people. Using a racial epithet, he told them to "get down there and get that boat unloaded." And they'd be strafed by gunfire. Knee High came back from the war, and his nerves were shot. He went to the VA for treatment, and he drank to calm his nerves.

I'd always ride down to the farm with Knee High and my daddy. We never spent a night at the farm, because Mama was a city girl. When Daddy died, Knee High sat right beside me at his service on Jan. 21, 1975.

All my ancestors fought for the Confederacy. I'm a member of the Sons of Confederate Veterans

(SCV) and the Military Order of the Stars and Bars. My maternal great-grandfather was a lieutenant in the Civil War. But color doesn't matter to me. Knee High was like a second father to me. He built me a tree house, and he built me a clubhouse. Knee High's daddy was nicknamed Big Hon (for Honey). He had a good job with the railroad, laying railroad tracks. Knee High lived with his mother and daddy. Big Hon always wore brand new-bib overalls. Knee High's mother, Mrs. Ferguson, had a good laugh.

Daddy and I went hunting one time at Thanksgiving, and I got a squirrel. We stopped by the Fergusons' house, and Daddy gave the squirrel to Mrs. Ferguson. Daddy said to them, "Just cut off the tail and put it on Knee High's pillow."

In the 1950s, Knee High would eat his lunch in the basement in the winter and outside in summer. In the summer, I would eat my lunch outside with him. The Salisbury Post would be delivered and I would run out and get it and give it to Knee High. He would always read the sports section to me. I loved hearing about Mickey Mantle, Yogi Berra, and the other New York Yankees.

One day, I vividly remember Knee High reading to me, and there was a picture on the front page of actor George Reeves in his Superman costume. I politely interrupted Knee High, and asked why

Superman was on the front page. Knee High told me Superman had killed himself. I couldn't believe it. Knee High said, "That's one bullet he didn't stop."

A couple of years before Daddy died, he got Knee High a job at Catawba in the janitorial department to get some retirement and build up his Social Security. He worked there eight to 10 years. He'd stop by occasionally and come see me. He never drove. He took the bus.

The man in the rain

Usually, my mom and I would go down with my dad to his big farm on High Rock Lake after Sunday School, church, and lunch at Mrs. Arey's boarding house. One Sunday, it was raining cats and dogs, so Mom said, "I believe I'll let y'all go down to the farm. I'm gonna stay here. The weather is too rough for me."

So Daddy and I put on some old clothes and got into our Pontiac and headed down to the farm. Daddy was going down the dirt road that was part of his farm. When I was a kid, it seemed to take forever to ride down that road. All of a sudden, my dad slammed on brakes and uttered a cuss word. I lunged forward in the car and looked up over the dashboard. There was a man lying in the road in the pouring rain with one of Daddy's prized hunting dogs licking his face. It was a man who worked on the farm. I didn't even know his name. He'd gotten drunk, let my dad's dogs loose, and passed out on the road in the rain.

Scared the dickens out of me. Daddy got out and went and got him up. I jumped in the back of the Pontiac and Daddy put him in the front seat. He drove the car over to the dog lot, got his whistle, rounded up all his dogs, and put them back into the dog lot. He took the man into the farmhouse and told him he had an hour to get off the property. That was the Southern way of alcohol rehabilitation. If you can't hold your liquor, get the hell off the property within an hour.

Another man who worked on the farm from time to time didn't show up for work one Monday. They called Daddy at the cotton office. Daddy got with the sheriff's department. Turned out the man had died that weekend. He got drunk and fell off the porch of a farmhouse — not ours, another one — and either broke his neck or drowned in the water from the downspout. They didn't know which it was. They just knew he was dead.

Workers on the farm

When my dad had his big farm he had an Allis-Chalmers tractor. I'd go down to the farm with Daddy every chance I got. He would go down whenever he was finished at the cotton brokerage office. I just loved it. He had people who lived in two houses there that worked on the farm. Lee Buck Poole didn't live there but he worked some for Daddy. Brownie, our Chesapeake Bay Retriever, stayed down there. Daddy's hunting dogs stayed here in town. He had some pretty high-dollar dogs, and I think he wanted them up here, close at hand.

Daddy would say, "Do you want to go out with Lee Buck?" Or Mike or Ode, or whoever was plowing. I'd get up on the tractor with them and just ride and ride and ride as we plowed row after row after row.

Lee Buck and all of them were in World War II and all of them had tattoos. Lee Buck was in the Pacific Theater. In the spring when he was plowing, he'd just have his bib overalls — no undershirt — work boots, and a hat. He had tears in the overalls, and I could see tattoos of hula dancers on both thighs. I could see the top of another on his chest. I thought that was really interesting. Between plowing and looking at the hula girls, I was happy. Every time we went over a bump, one of the hula dancers would jiggle.

After riding on the tractor with Lee Buck and seeing his tattoos, I decided I needed a few. I told my long-suffering mother. Looking at me in total disbelief, Mama said, "All right, whenever you see a child with a tattoo, let me know and we'll talk about it."

Several weeks later, Mama and I were out shopping. When it was my turn to go to the dime store, a dwarf walked out of Woolworths with tattoos on both arms.

"Mama, Mama!" I tugged at her dress and begged her to turn around and look at the now departing dwarf. By the time Mama finally turned around, the dwarf had gotten into a car and left.

"What was it you wanted me to see, Happy?"

"Nothing now."

Damn the bad luck.

Daddy had a GMC flat-bed truck down at the farm. I remember one day — I guess the following winter — we went to File's Store. Ode, Mike, Lee Buck, and I all got in the cab of the truck and rode from the farm to File's Store on Bringle Ferry Road. I was just 7, so I couldn't see over the dash.

I'd also never seen a clutch before. I thought there were two brake pedals. I was fascinated to see the gears change. The pedals were not rectangular but round.

Anyway, it was payday, I think, so we all went to File's, and Daddy had given me enough money to get a Brownie drink and some hoop cheese. They gave me some saltines. They always had an outdoor fire going in the back and empty cans of motor oil were stacked behind the store.

Lee Buck bought two packs of hot dogs, buns and mustard, and a six-pack of Pepsi-Colas. He put the hot dogs on a stick and warmed them up in the fire. He ate and drank all of it. I couldn't believe he could eat two packages of hot dogs — 10 to a pack — the buns and the Pepsis, all in one sitting. I sat there Indian-style watching Lee Buck, and I thought, "He is really something."

The last time I saw Lee Buck, I was 15 and had gone to see Bob and Lillie Starnes. Lee Buck stopped by and he was selling peaches. I remember my dad asked, "What are you getting for those peaches?" and Lee Buck said, "Fifty cents a peck."

Ode and Mabel Basinger worked on the farm. She always fixed me sweet tea with lemon. They never had children, so she made over me. She'd wash her dishes in the sink that had an old pump handle. I'd take my little model boat out there and play in a puddle she'd make when she tossed the water off the back porch.

Ode was a bombardier in WWII in Army Air Corps. He gave me his bombardier patch and the paraphernalia he brought back from Europe. Mike was Ode's brother. He was divorced and lived in the other house on the farm. He was a really neat guy, quiet, with jet-black hair. I remember roasting peanuts with Mike. We'd sit there and crack them open and eat them, then toss the shells on the ground.

Mike served in the Army in WWII. Ode, Mike, and Dick were all brothers. I only met Dick a couple of times. He worked on the farm off and on. They were all nice guys.

Mr. Hinson was a man who lived on the farm when Daddy purchased it. Daddy wanted me to spend time with him as I grew older, but Mr. Hinson died when I was about 4. Daddy said there was nothing in the woods that Mr. Hinson didn't know about. He knew all about plants and animals. I don't remember him at all, except what Daddy told me. He said he would have never sold the farm had Mr. Hinson lived. He thought that much of him. I wish I knew more to say about Mr. Hinson. Daddy thought the world of him. Daddy's main purpose in having the farm was for him and his buddies to hunt. They would also play cards down there. Daddy grew corn and hay. He bought all of his equipment from Bud and Red Troxler at Southern Implement in Spencer. It was a sad day for me when Daddy sold the farm.

"He drove the car into the river"

Bill Musselman was one of my dad's poker buddies. He was a collegiate wrestler in the mid-'40s. He and his wife and two daughters moved to Salisbury from Minnesota, where his family had a big farm. He was a strong, muscular guy. His daughters were probably 10 years older than I was, but I remember they were gorgeous. He and his family lived over near City Lake.

I remember one time they played cards down at High Rock. Daddy had a few drinks and so he rode home with somebody and left his car down there. My mother noticed the next day that Daddy was sleeping late. She noticed Daddy's car wasn't there so she called Bill.

"Bill, where is Harold's car?"

"He drove it into the river."

He didn't, of course, but it upset my mother, and Daddy didn't think too much of it when he heard it. Mother had a great sense of humor, but that one did not hit her right.

The micro midget

The micro midget racecar was made by Wayne Eddleman of Eddleman's Cycle and Machine Shop in China Grove. I was so small they had to put the pedals under the steering wheel and the brake lever on the side.

I got it for Christmas in 1956. I had written Santa Claus and asked for one. My dad had a garage and a little area in the back to cure country hams — and probably stash a little booze.

One day, I got to thinking, "If I were to get a micro midget where would it be? I bet it would be back in the garage."

So I went and looked, and there it was! I didn't let on that I knew it, though.

That Christmas morning, we had pancakes, and then my dad took me out and showed me the micro midget. He cranked it up and showed me how to work throttle and brake. I shot up through the yard with my 4-hp motor in the engine. It slid sideways and bumped my grandfather's house near his bedroom. He came out and looked at me with a stern look on his face. So I shot back toward Mom and Daddy's house.

It would go 35 mph, I remember that. They used to race them at Ellis Crossroads. My dad and I went out a couple of times on Friday nights and watched the race. I really enjoyed that.

But the Christmas morning I got my micro midget, we went to Hamlet as usual, where my mother's mother lived. My aunts and uncles from Richmond, Va., and Washington, D.C., would come. Dad put it in the trunk of the car and took it down there and cranked it up.

I took it out in the street driving. One of the neighbors called the police, and the police stopped me about two blocks from my grandmother's house and followed me back. So that was the end of riding the micro midget that day.

I never found out who ratted me out.

I kept it 'til I outgrew it, and then I got a go-kart, then a car. So I've always craved excitement.

On to go-karts

I loved my micro midget and I drove it all around the yard, but it was tearing up the grass. Daddy had a crew come in and put a track in the backyard, which was basically a sidewalk laid in a rectangular setup. I got really good at going around it at full speed. If you do something enough, you get good at it, if you're any count at all.

Around the cemetery
Locke Long, Jr. shares this story

Everybody couldn't afford micro midgets, so we got go-karts. Anywhere there was an opportunity, we'd have us a go-kart race. That was about as much fun as kids could have. We liked racing — NASCAR racing — and we had our own little vehicles. Hap would ride it to my house on the street.

I lived on the corner of Parkview Circle and Grove Street, across from the cemetery. We ran the go-karts around the cemetery and really had fun, until one of the neighbors complained. They told us we were desecrating the dead, and we had to stop running the go-karts. We didn't even know what that meant. Plus, they were dead. But we found other places.

Trouble with the micro midget

One day, I was riding the micro midget by myself in the backyard and the throttle stuck. I had it wide open.

Rather than end up in East Spencer, I decided I'd better run the car into the garage. So when I got to the garage, my head hit the cast-iron steering wheel, and I broke my nose. I didn't know I'd broken my nose. It just bled. The micro midget was not hurt. It was a real sturdy vehicle.

Over the years, I noticed I had trouble breathing through my nose. Finally, I went to Dr. Leighanne Dorton, a local ENT. She and my daughter, Heather, are friends.

She said, "I've never seen a nasal passage so out of line as yours."

In the summer of 2017, I had surgery to have it corrected. They called it a split septum, so she did corrective surgery. It's much better. I'm not 100 percent, but I'm much better than what I was.

Before my surgery, I told my friend Vick Bost that I had a "split rectum." He died laughing.

I had a nice suite at Novant. When I came out of surgery, I was in the room alone. The device to change the channel and call the nurses was all one piece. There was a Lifetime movie that had just started. I tried reaching to get the remote and it fell to the floor.

I couldn't ring for the nurses or change the channel 'til someone came in.

Still feeling the effects of the medicine, I couldn't move, so I just had to lie there and watch Lifetime for an hour. I guess the medication had weakened my brain, and before I knew it, I was crying about this girl whose husband had left her for two women. Looking back, it could have been double vision since I was on heavy medication. (Don't tell anyone this story.)

Actually, I have watched Lifetime a couple of times since. I'm not a Lifetime guy, but that experience in the hospital forced me to watch it.

The Big Game

We played baseball at McDaniel Field every single day in the summer. At night, we'd play organized Little League, and I was on the First Presbyterian team.

We had talked about this pick-up baseball game for a couple of weeks. We had Locke Long, Jr., Chris Agner, Doo-Doo Raynor, myself, the neighborhood bully, and other neighborhood kids. I guess we were all in the fifth grade. It was a good game.

The team I was on was ahead by a run and it was getting close to the end of the game. My cousin Kent Roberts had broken his arm a couple of months earlier. He had his arm wrapped, but had still ridden his bicycle to watch the game. To even the score up some, we decided that we'd let Kent play for the losing team. About that time, Knee High came up in his nice, good-looking suit, with one of Daddy's nice dress hats, and he'd been drinking a little bit. He and Daddy had probably been talking about 30 minutes. We went over and said, "Knee High, if you don't mind, can you pitch for the other team, to even up things?"

The team that was behind took Kent, and he came to the plate. There were two outs and two men on base. Knee High warmed up. We had a hard ball. It was fast pitch. One of his pitches went one way and one went the other. I was concerned because he was on my team. He warmed up, then he started concentrating. Took his coat off. Took his hat off. You could just see his muscles bulging.

And I thought to myself, "I'm damn glad I'm not Kent Roberts facing Knee High pitching at me."

Doo-Doo was playing center field, which was way back toward the edge of 115 Merritt, my parents' house. The driveway between 115 and 117 was "center field," and if it went over there, it was a home run.

Well, Knee High threw a strike, Kent swung and missed. The next pitch, two guys on base, you know, nervous, they were wanting to get in there, tie the score and then win with the winning run. Knee High threw a good, fast ball, but Kent stood right up to the plate — broken arm and all — and swung at it. And knocked the heck out of that ball.

But you could see Jimmy "Doo-Doo" Raynor running back toward the driveway. He had one of his brother Voodoo's old first baseman mitts. It was just a rag of a glove. Jimmy kept running, held the glove up, and he caught the ball. He fell down and rolled over, and then held his glove up. He had retained the ball.

The runners quit going around. Our team had won by one run. Knee High was happy. His team had won, but he was happy before he got there. Kent was proud of the ball he hit. It was great, but Doo-Doo just outran it and made one of the most fantastic catches since Willie Mays, I guess. That was The Big Game.

One last footnote: My mother had cooked hot dogs for us before the game. And my mother didn't like any kind of pork — she thought it needed to have the heck cooked out of it. And I just could hardly eat the hot dogs because they didn't have any taste. Chris Agner bragged on them and ate three. But anyway, that was The Great Baseball Game. And I'll never forget Doo-Doo running back there, his limp ol' first baseman glove hanging up there, looking at the ball, running as fast as he could, catching it, falling down, rolling, and holding up the ball that he'd retained. Heckuva game.

Voodoo and Doo-Doo

Growing up in the mid-'50s was really neat around here, because the area was full of kids. We've mentioned Doo-Doo Raynor and the Big Game.

George went by "G" and his dad was editor of the Salisbury Post. Every time somebody got in trouble, it seemed like G was always around. He got the nickname "Voodoo." Then Jimmy got the nickname "Doo-Doo" because it rhymed with "Voodoo."

Doo-Doo and I were out playing catch one day and the neighborhood bully came over and started picking on us. Let's call him Bobby. So Jimmy picked up a board that had a rusty nail in it and hit him in the butt with it. That made Bobby mad, my God in heaven! Jimmy and I took off running. I was in the lead and Jimmy followed. Where the man cave is now was our route. We wanted to go up in the loft and close the door. I used part of a conveyor belt as a ladder and we'd go up there and close the door. Bobby said for us to come down and he'd kick our butts.

Yeah, we were going down there. Jimmy took a stack of hardwood flooring Daddy had stored up there and pushed it through the opening. If it would have hit Bobby in the head it would have killed him. The flooring had metal bands around it, and they popped open like they were rubber bands. Wood went everywhere.

Bobby left.

When we were sure he was gone, we came out. We picked up all the wood. I didn't want the wrath of Daddy, so we picked it up and stored it back up there.

Voodoo and the pool game

Kent Roberts and I were talking recently about Voodoo. Kent took me up to Ed Rufty's pool hall once when I was 12. He was 16 and had just started driving. Voodoo was in a clandestine 9-ball tournament. Voodoo was nervous. He trembled. His opponent won four straight matches until he finally missed a ball. Damn. Good play. Voodoo then stood up and played. He ran the table for 10 straight games. His opponent conceded, and Voodoo went around to all the pockets and collected his money.

The man chosen to rack the balls each game was Mr. Charlie Butler. Ed Rufty met him in Las Vegas in the 1940s when Mr. Butler played 9-ball at $10,000 per game.

Ed Rufty's pool hall

Ed Rufty was Archie Rufty's brother. He graduated from N.C. State with a degree in textiles. But I knew him as the owner of Ed's Pool Hall, where I learned to play pool. Kent Roberts, my cousin and longtime mentor, introduced me to Ed when I was 14. Kent also taught me to shoot pool.

Ed had three men who worked for him, racking balls and selling soft drinks and snacks. Charlie Butler was his number-one man. The second in command was a man called Sambo. I don't know his last name. He was a white guy and always wore khaki pants. I can't remember the third man's name. All were nice guys and would help us learn pool as best we would listen.

Every Christmas, Ed would open the pool hall and everybody could shoot pool for free. I went up there several Christmases with Kent until he went off to college.

Ed Rufty was truly a nice guy. He had a nickname for all of us. Mine was Towne Pharmacy because I worked there. What a lousy nickname! Kent was Wolfpack, another guy was Morrisono, another guy Slade. And me Towne Pharmacy. Ugh!

The pond, the cave, and the copperhead

In 68 years, I haven't moved much geographically. Back in the 1950s, my parents' house was down where our offices are. My office, controller Wanda Peffer's office and facility manager Charles Church's office are all in Aunt Mabel's house. Krispy Kreme sits on the site of my grandparents' house. Jeanette Lassiter's office is in the apartments, and the other houses I've bought over the years belonged to our neighbors and now serve to insulate the campus.

After WWII, there were kids everywhere in this neighborhood. I met my best friend for life, Locke Long, Jr., in the 2-year-old class at First Presbyterian Church. He later went to State, and I went to Catawba. When we were growing up, he was either coming to my house or I was going to his. Where Moose Pharmacy is now was a shortcut from my parents' house to Locke's house. The neighborhood kids made a pond up there. The older kids went to City Park, caught fish in the lake, then brought them over to the pond. We would try to catch the fish there a second time.

It was overgrown around the pond. Rowan Dairy was nearby, and old equipment had been thrown out behind it. That's where I got my little piece of conveyor belt that became my ladder for various adventures. The dairy had also thrown concrete slabs back there which became our cave. You could only crawl so far back there. Luckily, no one got stuck, but it was pretty creepy. There was also the occasional snake — a black snake or a copperhead.

The shortcut was not my favorite route. I had to avoid copperheads or the occasional bully. I had to cut through three backyards and sometimes one of the old people would yell at me for cutting through.

I got the bright idea of walking down Merritt Avenue and turning right on Parkview Circle. What is now another house on campus used to belong to a family we'll call the Millers. They had two mean daughters. I could ride my bike down Parkview when I was 7 or 8. If they saw me, they would pull me off my bike and sit on me. After a couple of thrashings from the Miller sisters, I decided to take my chances on the copperheads. Less poison.

In the other direction, I'd go see Kee Kirchin, my good friend on Mahaley Avenue. I'd ride my bike in the other direction on Parkview, and turn right on Mahaley. When I got to Kee's house, I'd get off the bike and walk it across the street. There were two mean girls down on that end of the road. Let's call them the Shaver sisters. They'd do the same thing — stop me and pull me off the bike and sit on me. They were older than the Miller sisters.

One morning after breakfast, I was going over to Kee's, and here came the Shaver girls, bouncing out of their house. One of them had a half grapefruit she didn't want for breakfast. One sister held me and one did an "Edward G. Robinson" in my face with the grapefruit. In the 1931 movie, "The Public Enemy," Edward G. Robinson and his girlfriend were sitting at a table in a movie and he did it to her.

I didn't have a shortcut from my house to Kee's, so I had to improvise a route to avoid the Shaver sisters. I'd ride on the sidewalk down Innes, cut through Ketner Center, and get on the sidewalk from Ketner Center to Kee's. It was longer, but it was much less painful and humiliating.

The $100,000 bills

When I was 5 or 6, I'd go uptown with my mother, and we'd go to the dime store. I always wanted one or two things, either little plastic Army soldiers, or play money. I had right much of both. I'd store them under my bed. There were two kids who lived in the duplex where Moose Pharmacy is now. Uncle Wilbur owned it. When I was 6, Jimmy was 4 and his younger brother Edwin was 3. There was a girl who lived in my parents' apartments who was my age. We were swinging one time, and the girl asked me if I could get Jimmy and Edwin to take their clothes off and swing.

As luck would have it, Jimmy and Edwin came down there. I said, "I've gotta talk these guys into swinging." I went back to the girl and said, "Are you sure you want me to ask them to do that?" and she said, "Yeah." So I went inside and got several $100,000 bills with Donald Duck on the front. I said, "I'll give you $100,000 if you'll go behind that bush and take your clothes off and come back and swing, so Girl A can see."

They said, "Wow! OK!" Then she said, "Can you get them to jump off the swing?" And I gave them $100,000 and they did that. I thought that was the end of the story, but the story was just beginning.

Trouble lurked around the corner.

There used to be a Rowan Dairy down here. You could get ice cream cones, a nickel a scoop, and milkshakes, 25 cents. You could buy a gallon of milk. Everybody drank milk back then. This was the mid-'50s.

Girl A went home. Jimmy and Edwin looked like they were heading home, but instead, they went down to the Rowan Dairy and ordered milkshakes. And when the cashier asked for a quarter, they plopped down $100,000 bill with Donald Duck on it. That didn't fly, and they didn't have any other money.

Unfortunately, Jimmy knew his family's phone number. Their mother went down there and paid for the milkshakes. They went home crying. Their mother grilled them, and they couldn't keep their mouths shut. They spilled the beans. Next thing I know, Mother is yelling at me. Jimmy and Edwin's mama had called her and told her the whole story. Mama was really upset with me. She said, "I'm going to call your daddy at the office."

Back then, you had one phone in the center of the house. I remember holding her leg, her dragging me to the phone, me crying at this point. Shortly thereafter, here comes the big Pontiac with the big engine and the big man in it. He said, "Idell, get me the yardstick." At that point, I composed myself, broke free of my mama, and ran and hid under my bed. I think I blacked out. The last thing I remember is seeing the yardstick, just missing my face. I remember thinking, "Well, maybe I could live under here. Maybe I could have a pallet and hear television from the living room." I tried to make the best of it.

Their nerves finally healed. I think I was banned from buying money after that. I had to stick to plastic Army men.

One summer, Jimmy, Edwin, and I were playing together in the backyard. Daddy was at the office or the farm. Mama had gone downtown shopping. This was in the '50s, but they had locked the door. I wanted to go into the house and get some toys out. So did Jimmy and so did Edwin. So I got my trusty conveyor ladder and put Edwin on the roof. We told him to go down the chimney and unlock the door.

We tried coaxing him to go down the chimney. We thought Santa Claus did it. He was able to go to the peak and look down.

I said, "Go ahead, Santa Claus does it!"

He said, "It's dark! I can't see anything!"

Thank God he came down. That was one tragedy that didn't happen, and we couldn't blame it on Girl A.

The Soap Box Derby, lemonade stand, and Wachovia Bank

In 1959, the Soap Box Derby was a big deal. That year it was held on Grove Street in Salisbury on a hot July day. My best friend for life, Locke Long, Jr., and I set up a lemonade stand in front of their house on Grove Street. With help from his mother, Ruby, and sisters, Marianna and Jean, we had not only the best lemonade but the only lemonade available that day. Even longtime Salisburian Norman Ingle came by our stand and yelled a song to the crowd.

"Hey, get your cold lemonade! Made in the shade, stirred with a spade available right here!"

At the end of the day, I made two dollars and change. I kept the change but took the two dollars up to the new Wachovia Bank branch and opened a savings account. In January, I took my savings book up to the bank and put a dollar in from Christmas. The cashier gave back my book and I had three dollars and 2 cents. Sweet! 2 cents, my first interest income! I loved it.

Years later after other deposits, I took money out of that account and bought my first 50 shares of Food Town Stores, Inc.

Families in the neighborhood

The Hardisters had a son, Jay, who was an only child like me. He and maybe six other boys in the neighborhood were much older — and bigger — than Locke and me. My dad bought me a set of soapbox derby wheels and an axle. I had no plans to build a soapbox derby car, so Knee High built me a scooter or a coaster, as I called it. He used the wheels and axle, then made me a seat and put a board across the bottom where I could prop my feet, and tied a rope around the front axle so I could steer.

I would take it to the top of the driveway and slowly coast down the hill and turn into the front of the apartments. I'd do this over and over and over. I had a dog named Hoby, named for a mean man in a Western TV show. Hoby would run behind me, and it was wonderful.

When I was born, my family called me Happy. By the time I was 7, I preferred Hap.

Well, Jay Hardister and a couple of big guys walking down Merritt Avenue saw me. I was 7, and they were 14.

Jay hollered, "Hey Happy, let's see that thing go faster."

I said, "No, thanks, I'm doing just fine."

They said, "C'mon."

They got the cart by the rope and took me up to my grandfather's house. They made me get in it and pushed me as fast as they could go and let me go about the front of the apartment house. I was flying.

I mean, I was flying.

I came to the intersection of Parkview and Merritt. I didn't know exactly what to do. So I tried turning it to the left and the thing jerked. The left wheel went up underneath the cart and threw me out. I scraped my left thumb and you could see the scar for years after.

I escaped tragedy once again!

Bill and Mabel Barringer lived across the street from where the apartments are. They never had any children.

Mr. Barringer served in WWI in France. He said it was absolutely horrible. He was thinking about going AWOL when the Armistice was signed. Barringer Street is named for him. He owned that house and the lot beside him, which he sold to the folks who ended up having Bobby, our neighborhood bully.

Rip Hale lived in the house I recently bought. It's the second house down from Jeanette's office at the apartment house. Rip was a neat kid. He was an only child and had an uncle who'd been in WWII. They dedicated an entire bedroom to a Lionel train set his uncle had given him. Every birthday and Christmas and any other special occasion, he got a Lionel accessory to add to it. We all coveted his train set. It was fabulous.

I don't know where his dad worked, but he got transferred out of town, and they moved in the late 1950s.

Goodbye, Rip. Goodbye, Lionel train set.

The Bouknights owned the house beside the apartment house. They were an older couple who didn't have any children.

Wrestling was big back in the '50s, and they'd catch a taxi every Wednesday night to see live wrestling at the old Charlotte Coliseum with Big Bill Ward and Jim Crockett as the announcer and promoter. Mr. and Mrs. B. would buy a bottle of liquor, take a cab to the bus station, ride the bus down to Charlotte, watch the wrestling match, then take the bus home, followed by a taxi. All the while, they'd be sipping on the liquor. They were the first people I knew to drink and not drive, which was smart.

Karen Thomas was my first girlfriend. She lived in my parents' apartment house. Her parents were Bob and Arva Thomas. They were a great family. I thought she was great. We were probably 4, and we played together in the neighborhood. Then they moved to Morganton, and I was so sad to see the moving truck come. But we had a lot of fun.

Daddy had a tool box he always kept locked. When he sold the farm, he moved it to a little nook in his garage. I've got the toolbox now. It's in the roadhouse. I don't know how old it is. It's made of wood treated with oil.

I took all the tools out and have some knickknacks of my stuff in there. It ties me to my dad and means a lot to me. I wouldn't take anything for it. Nothing fancy, but a lot of memories there.

The talent show

We had a talent show when we were in sixth grade at Frank B. John Elementary School in Mrs. Grace Mesimer's class. My friend Michael Freedman said, "We need to get together and do something for the talent show. We need to do something where we throw a cream pie at you or me."

We also enlisted Chris Agner and Locke Long, Jr. We got a copy of the record, "I'm Looking Over a Four Leaf Clover" by Mitch Miller's Band. We played it over and over and over and learned the words to it.

We asked Mrs. Mesimer if she would let Mrs. Betty Driscoll, the music teacher, come and play the piano while we sang. As far as they were concerned, we were just going to stand and sing "I'm Looking Over a Four Leaf Clover," while

Mrs. Driscoll played.

The rest of the story is … we got a pie shell and filled it full of shaving cream. Michael was dressed in regular school clothes, but the other three of us dressed as hobos. When it was our turn, we walked out on stage, and I turned around and directed the other two guys while Mrs. Driscoll played.

Michael came out, skipping around like he was sweeping the floor. I grabbed him and took him off stage while the other two kept singing.

Michael came out with the pie in his hand, and he was sorta tip-toeing. When the young children saw Michael, they screamed with delight. The three of us were onstage singing the song. Michael tapped me on the shoulder and was holding the pie up like he was gonna throw it at me. But I pointed up to the balcony, Michael looked up, and I grabbed the pie and hit him in the face. We had practiced our parts over and over and over. The music ended perfectly.

Now, the main competition we had was the other sixth-grade class, and they had memorized "Casey at the Bat." They had one girl who had memorized the poem, and the kids were behind her acting it out. It was boring, but they spent a lot of time practicing. Theirs was art. Ours was fun, fun, fun.

The winner was chosen by applause, and we were the last to go back out on stage. The auditorium roared with delight. They clapped and cheered and yelled. They gave us a plaque. There was nothing the teachers could do. We had overwhelming approval. The girl who memorized "Casey at the Bat" was behind stage crying.

We were walking on air. Our teacher was just smirking the whole time. But one of the teachers from the lower grades came up and said, "My class wonders if your group who did the hobo show could come down and speak to our class a moment." So we walked down with the teacher and spoke to her fourth-grade class. So we went to every other classroom, too. We walked in, and we were like rock stars.

We didn't have a name for our act. We just called it, "I'm Looking Over a Four Leaf Clover."

We got away with murder, and the kids loved it.

We didn't have a school bus. They were just out in the county. We took the city bus to go home from school. After the talent show that day, we didn't change our clothes before we got on the bus. It stopped by Catawba on the way home. Back in the 1950s, there were a bunch of Yankees who went to Catawba.

One of them said, "What are you dressed up for?"

We told them we'd been in a talent show.

The guy said, "That's some talent, dressing up like hobos."

When we got off the bus, we all said, "Damn Yankees."

We always wondered what it would be like to go the entire route on the bus. One time we got on the bus and told the bus driver what we wanted to do. He said, "It'll cost you an extra nickel, but I'll give you a transfer."

So we went the entire route, all the way out to East Spencer and back by Catawba and the VA, and to the Square. I thought it was marvelous. The driver let us get off at the Square and go into Purcell's Drug Store to get a paper cone of water. We gently took it back on the bus. It took us about an hour. It was glorious. It was fun. We didn't have anything we had to do that afternoon, other than homework. So we rode the bus.

My best friend for life

Locke Long, Jr. is my lifelong friend and best friend forever. We had so much fun together growing up. We camped out as boys. He's a great Boy Scout leader in Charlotte. He's trained about 110 Eagle Scouts.

His great-grandfather was the first surgeon in North Carolina. His grandfather was the head of the Long Sanitarium in Statesville, the first big hospital there. He had an uncle who for years was the only doctor in Mocksville. His other uncle, a dentist in Statesville, lived in the family home place and built his practice next door.

Locke Long, Sr. went to Carolina for a couple of years, then went into the insurance business. He had an office above where Jimmy and Gordon Hurley's office is now on West Innes Street. We loved riding up to see his dad on our bikes. We'd look out the window to the Capitol Theatre and watch the happenings on the street.

Mr. Long was a member of the auxiliary police force. One time when we were up there, he had a couple of policemen there, and they were talking and cutting up. The lady who ran the concession stand at the theater had gone to Purcell Drug Co. and purchased some items. She wasn't very attractive, and she was waddling back down the sidewalk with two bags in her arms.

All of a sudden, Mr. Long yelled, "Hap!"

I wondered what I had done wrong.

He said it again.

"Hap! Get off the street! Here comes your girlfriend!"

Locke married a lady whose father owned a custom filter manufacturing company. Locke went into sales with them and eventually took over the company. He and I talk occasionally. We've sort of lost contact, with him being in Charlotte and me being here. We stayed in touch more when his dad was alive. We'd go out to lunch at College Barbecue, or if we had time, we went down to Gary's.

But I can pick up the phone and call him and have the greatest conversation. Like me, he is still working.

When I was about 11, I had a magazine with an ad on the back cover. The guy was wearing thick glasses and looking at a woman. He could see her shapely body because he was wearing X-ray glasses.

I said, "Well, hell, I'd like to get some of these." I ordered a pair and thought they'd be in before school was out so I could look at a couple of girls in class. But they didn't come in time.

Well, bless pat, my mother yelled up to me, "Hap! There's a package here for you from New York. What have you been up to?"

"Oh, I just ordered something out of a baseball magazine."

So, I ran downstairs and got the package, took it up to my room, and put them on. I looked around and I couldn't see any X-ray action. School was out. It was summertime. I thought, "I shouldn't do this, but maybe I could walk downstairs and see if I can see through my mother's clothes."

It was all research and development.

I walked down the steps and I was like Dr. Cyclops with these huge glasses on, plodding along. They were just magnifiers. I finally got downstairs and I walked into the kitchen quietly. My mother was bent over in front of the sink, putting some pots underneath the kitchen sink. I looked at her behind, and I couldn't see through her dress!

What a rip-off.

I ran upstairs and was grieving over the $4.50 I'd spent, plus 45 cents shipping and handling. So I did what any other red-blooded American boy would do.

I called Locke Long, Jr.

I said, "Hey, Locke! Guess what I've got? I've got some X-ray glasses and you can look through them and see nekkid ladies! I've seen about everybody I wanted to see, so if you want to see them I can sell them to you. If you've got $5 from shoveling snow over the winter, I've got a nickel I can give you and these glasses."

He said, "Yeah, bring 'em on over. I'd be interested in that."

We exchanged the money for the glasses. Then I rode my bicycle home as fast as I could. In about 15 minutes, the phone rang. I didn't answer it. It rang again. It rang a third time. I finally answered it, and it was Locke.

"How do you like the glasses?" I asked Locke.

"I don't care much for them," he said. "Did they work for you?"

"Yeah, I saw a couple of nekkid women. What

about you?"

"Well, Marianna and Jean (his younger sisters) were back in their bedroom playing with their dolls. I know I shouldn't have done it, but I didn't have anybody else to look at, so I put the glasses on and I went back there. Jean was dressing one of her dolls, and she was bent over."

"What did you see?"

"I saw a behind that looked about 3 feet wide."

I said, "Something must be wrong with them, because they were sure working for me!"

The neighborhood bully
Locke Long, Jr. shares this story

We ran from Bobby in fear for years. It was Hap's older, stronger cousin Kent we deferred to whenever Bobby got too close on us. We could always count on Kent. Bobby was afraid of Kent.

Why are people bullies? I don't know if it's ever that simple. We were easy to bully, of course, being years younger and half his weight. We were easy targets. Why he was a bully, I don't know. He cornered us up in the loft of Hap's father's garage one time. We were scared. We figured he wouldn't come up after us. We stayed up there like little mice in the attic until we thought the coast was clear. We got on our bikes and went to see Kent. Kent said, "I'll talk to him."

We never had any problems after we told Kent. He and Bobby knew each other well enough, so they must have been close in age. This all happened when Hap and I were little people. We were riding bikes.

Bobby didn't come to my side of the block. This all happened on Merritt Avenue where Hap lived. Once we got over on my side of the block, on Grove Street, we never had any trouble. He wouldn't follow us over there, so he wasn't a widespread bully. He wasn't malicious or anything. We were just easy to pick on.

Hap was a mess. Always has been. We always got along so well. We were like two pages out of the same book. Still are. Even though we don't see each other often. It doesn't matter how much time has passed. We're still best friends.

Fishing trip to Uncle John's farm
Locke Long, Jr. shares this story

Uncle John Long was my dad's older brother. He raised cattle and had a big farm just this side of Statesville. He had a long dirt road down to a pond with fish and turtles.

On Saturday afternoons, usually Hap and I rode with my dad. We'd take our fishing rods and our rifles. Sometimes we took our bicycles. But one Saturday morning, Hap and I got the notion we would ride our bicycles to Uncle John's. It was about 25 miles. Hap and I rode up to Dad's office, which we did all the time.

He said, "We're gonna ride up to Uncle John's and go fishing."

I'm sure my dad didn't think we'd really go.

He said, "OK, I'll see you later."

Hap and I rode by his house.

"I'm going up to Uncle John's with Locke," he told his mom.

She assumed we were riding with my father. We had the fishing rods and tackle boxes, and a rifle, and we got on our bicycles and headed out Highway 70 to Iredell County. We rode and we rode and we rode. We were maybe 12 or 13, maybe 14. Young teens.

Riding and riding and riding.

We got tired and a little hungry. We pulled into Wink's BBQ and we had to take a break. You had to water the worms. It was so hot we thought the worms were gonna die. So Hap went into the bathroom to water the worms. We got a long way off and Hap said, "Oh no, I forgot the worms."

"Go get them."

"I'm too tired."

He talked me into going back for the worms. He's a smooth talker — he always has been. I turned around, went back to Wink's, got the worms and caught up with Hap.

At sundown, we pulled up at Uncle John's farm. We had made it and the sun was going down. We didn't make it to the pond. We were running out of light. My father pulled into the dirt road. He put the bicycles in the trunk and ran us down to the pond. He had a big ol' Ford Galaxy. He said, "I'll be back in a little while."

We went fishing. Nobody made a big deal out of it. It didn't seem to surprise Dad.

What was he thinking? We made it! That's a long way for two little boys on one-speed bikes.

So that was the ride to Statesville. My wife thinks it's still pretty funny that Hap talked me into going back for the worms.

Playing Army

Mike Smith's dad was in WWII, and Mike was one of our Army buddies. Playing Army in this neighborhood was big, really big. I was one of the younger kids and Mike Smith, Bobby and Jay were older guys. Somehow, we all got along when we played Army.

There used to be a forest behind Food Town. Now it's just a grassy area. We would play there. We'd play near the pond and the cave. We'd have toy guns and shoot somebody and say, "I gotcha!" And they'd say "No, you didn't."

"Yes, I did."

"No, you didn't."

We'd climb trees and play sniper. We had a few patches our G.I. relatives brought home from the war, and we'd trade those and look at those. We might have some sergeant stripes and we'd coax our mothers into sewing them on an old shirt for us. Playing Army was big here.

Then in the summertime, walking up to McDaniel Field where Food Lion is now was big. It was an overgrown field near Merritt Avenue.

We would play at McDaniel Field during the day.

We'd play pick-up baseball, and at night we'd put on our uniforms and play for the church league or civic club teams: Optimist, Lions, Elk, Rockwell. The guys from Rockwell would whip our butts. They were good. The church league teams were First Presbyterian, First Baptist, First Methodist, and St. John's.

We had an all-star game about mid-July, where the best of the church league would play the best of the civic organizations. Everybody on the all-star team got to play — sort of like they do in the major leagues. I played in two all-star games at first base for First Presbyterian.

All the Little League games were free admission except for the all-star game: 50 cents for adults and children under 12 free. That went for upkeep of the facility.

On the fence were hand-painted signs by Mr. Harwood of Harwood Signs in Granite Quarry. (I think his son or grandson has it now.) One was Food Town. If you hit a homerun over that section of the fence, you got two T-bone steaks from Food Town.

Max Brockman

One of my dad's best hunting and fishing buddies was Max Brockman. Mr. Brockman was vice president of Southern Railroad back in the day. He was a big man, with long gray hair and a deep, strong voice. He and my dad would come in from a day of hunting quail on my dad's farm holding their bounty. I still remember seeing him standing in our living room with his hunting coat on, no boots, but rather leggings from his service in World War I.

"Hap, take these birds in to your mother," Mr. Brockman said. And I ran over and took his birds and my dad's bunch, and felt the feathery creatures, still warm in my hands.

My favorite memory of Mr. Brockman was a party he gave back in the early 1950s. He was one of the last railroad executives to have his own private rail car. It was parked on a side rail at the passenger station in Salisbury. The party was given on his railroad car, with 10 or so couples in attendance. I was the only child. Porters in white jackets were serving the adults hors d'oeuvres and cocktails, and cigarette smoke filled the car. Then we were all seated, and big steaks with all the trimmings were served to the guests. I remember my mother cutting my steak, and me eating it as I took in that magical night.

I will never forget that wonderful Southern gentleman. Truly a self-made man, one I wished I could have known better. What stories I would

have learned. I will always cherish that special
evening aboard Mr. Brockman's car.

Daddy, the Highway Patrol, and the fishing trip

Daddy was one of the first Highway Patrolmen
in North Carolina in the 1930s. I've tried to find
his diploma. Gov. Clyde Hoey and Thad Eure
both signed it. He had to learn all 100 counties in
the state. I think he had been in all 100 counties.
You did the whole state. He told me he could
be at the Outer Banks one day and Durham the
next. You drove whatever was available. He was
trained on a 1934 Indian motorcycle. They had
some confiscated cars from moonshiners they
could assign to you. After Papa got to where he
wasn't comfortable driving, he offered Daddy
a partnership in H.K. Roberts & Sons, which
was just starting to get off the ground. So Daddy
changed jobs.

In the 1960s, all the guys who had started out
with him were the top dogs in the Highway
Patrol. Daddy was a great driver. He could drive a
Pontiac through the eye of a needle. He always had
Pontiacs with the biggest engine in them. When
they introduced the Pontiacs with a 3 2-barrel
carburetor, he got one of those. They were fast. He
always had a coupe. He always kept his I.D. card
from the Highway Patrol. We would get pulled

over for speeding and I worried they were going to haul him off to jail. I looked in the rear-view mirror and the next thing I knew, they were laughing and patting each other on the shoulder. Then Daddy got back in the car and off we went.

I said, "Daddy did you get a ticket?"

He said, "No."

That went on until 1963, and Daddy had a 1961 Pontiac Bonneville, again with a 3 2-barrel carburetor. He was to go to Currituck Sound with a bunch of his friends. He had some appointments, so he couldn't ride down with them. He was going to catch up with them that night. That's before the big bridges, when they had ferries connecting the islands. So Daddy got on the ferry, with only a few people on there. He said to the ferry captain, "Is there any law enforcement on the island? I'm running late and I'm going to have to let this car rip to get there to get on down to Currituck Sound, and get up with the guys in time for supper."

The guy piloting the boat said, "No, there's no one there." So Daddy let the thing rip. And about that time, on down the line, a siren came on. This Highway Patrol officer wasn't one of the good ol' boys. He was a freshly installed Highway Patrolman. He told Daddy pretty quick he didn't give a damn what he did in the 1930s with the Highway Patrol. He asked Daddy if he knew how fast he was going. Daddy said, "No, I don't." He said, "I clocked you at 105 miles an hour."

So, welcome to the new fellas on the Highway Patrol force. No more free passes.

Daddy and his friends went to Currituck. Twice a year they would fish one trip, then duck hunt the next trip. Each night, they would play poker. They had excellent cooks — all black ladies — at the fishing lodge where they stayed.

They especially thought a lot of one of the cooks. Her congregation was building a new church down there. Nothing fancy. One of the nights down there they decided to donate whatever was in the pot when they shut down the poker game. I think she got a pretty nice little penny there.

Years later, some of the younger people in that group were in their 50s and 60s when I was in my 30s, retired from Food Town. My father had been dead 10 years.

A couple of them said, "We want you to come with us fishing at Currituck. We're going to take you where your dad used to go. One guide there always tells a story about Harold Roberts. He really thought a lot of your dad."

So I went with them — Bill Sherrill, Locke Long, Sr., Bob Chandler, Buck Faison, and others. We were assigned boats and Buck was having some heart issues. I didn't care about casting all day long. I said, "I'll go with Buck." Buck was my kind of fisherman. He told the guide to go over and tie us to a dock of a house that was unoccupied during that time of the season. We went over and ate our lunch out of the lunchbox. Buck reared back and took a nap. This was my kind of fishing.

There's nobody in the world who knows more jokes than these fishing guides. Our guide started telling jokes and I'd die laughing, and he'd tell stories and I would die laughing. When he wasn't a fishing guide, he'd work as a roofer. It was more fun than a barrel of monkeys, being tied up to the dock, Buck taking a nap and the guide telling story after story. I drank a few beers. The guide drank a few of Buck's beers because Buck was asleep. We had the biggest time.

We had wonderful meals. We had huge country breakfasts, served about 4:30 a.m. The cooks would prepare our lunch. They'd put us two sandwiches in there, potato chips and two soft drinks. We would fish 'til lunch time, eat our lunch and fish some more. Then we'd come back, shower, and have social time. We would meet in somebody's room — they called it the "drinking room" — and then we would talk and have a couple of drinks. Then we'd have the most fabulous country dinner you could imagine: fried chicken, cooked cabbage, peas with homemade bread for breakfast and supper. The final night, we had steaks, baked potatoes, and salad. Then the ladies cut off all the lights in the dining room and brought out bananas foster, flaming, to the center of the table. It was a fisherman's dream week.

After the second or third night, Locke Long, Sr. said, "I want to take you to meet a man who used to be your dad's guide. He always asks about people in Salisbury, and he really hated to hear when your dad died."

So we went down there, about five miles from the fishing lodge. By this time, the man had gone blind. He had a nice, little brick house with a screened-in porch. And Mr. Long and the man and I went out on the porch and talked. He said, "I thought so much of your father. He was a fine gentleman, and I sure miss him coming down here."

I really appreciated Locke Long, Sr. taking me down there, and introducing me to him, and us sitting and talking. That was enjoyable.

I only went once, and I thoroughly enjoyed it. I've talked to many people in my dad's age group, and everybody had a story to tell.

Cuba before Castro

Life was never dull growing up as Harold and Idell's son. Just like Papa and Uncle Wilbur, Daddy read each day. The Greensboro Daily News, The Charlotte Observer, The Wall Street Journal, and The Salisbury Post — cover to cover, word for word. He could take a pop quiz on all and pass with flying colors.

One morning at the breakfast table in 1956, Daddy said we all needed to get down to Havana before Batista fell. He wanted to catch a big marlin and go to the night spots. Mama wasn't too crazy about it. I was all in. The second grade hadn't dismissed for summer break, and she didn't want me missing school for a trip to Cuba. I couldn't believe it! Mama was adamant. I wasn't going. I talked to Daddy and promised if he could get me a babysitter who spoke English I could keep up with my studies. All to no avail. Mama and I were staying home and Daddy would come back from Cuba and update us on the situation there.

Two weeks later, Daddy arrived home safe and sound from Havana. His suitcase was full of neat stuff, some of the trappings of his trip. He had two nice suits made in Havana and I'm sure many stories suitable for his poker buddies. None for Mama and me. Dammit. Years later, he passed those beautiful suits on to Knee High.

First Presbyterian Church

I've been a lifelong member of First Presbyterian Church. Angie Barker was in my kindergarten Sunday School class. We had beads to play with. After our Sunday School lesson, we'd count little wooden (probably lead-painted) beads, combining an educational activity with Sunday School.

On Sunday morning, Angie stuck a bead up her nose, and the teacher couldn't get it out. They called Dr. McCutcheon.

He said, "Bring her up to the Wallace Building, and I will meet her at my office."

The assistant teacher, Miss Mildred Lyerly, took her up there in her car. Miss Chene, our teacher, gathered us into a circle. We went around the circle and prayed for Angie to get that bead out of her nose. It was traumatic. I dreamed she never got the bead out, and she'd have to breathe out of one nostril. It was traumatic for all of us. We kept thinking about it.

Another boy swallowed a dime. We'd pass the plate around every Sunday, and while he was waiting, he stuck his dime in his mouth to hold it and somehow swallowed it.

All of the children heard the teacher talk to his mother, "Be sure and check his bowel movements the next few days. Use a fork to see if you can find it."

I couldn't use a fork for about three months.

I also went to first grade at the First Presbyterian Church. I went to Frank B. John Elementary School in second grade, and that's when Ralph Ketner moved back to Salisbury and started Food Town. His daughter, Linda, was in my class. I noticed tears coming down her cheeks one day. The only thing I had in my pocket was an empty cartridge from a .22-caliber Hornet rifle. I walked over and gave her that spent cartridge and she stopped crying. I was sort of her buddy after that. We talked about that when her dad was sick. She said she wished she still had that cartridge.

I was out of town, but I called one of my guys in the IT department. I had him special order some .22 Hornet cartridges. They're hard to come by. I told him, "Go up to my office, use your key to get in my closet, get the .22 Hornet rifle out, take it out to the Rifle Club and shoot four cartridges and bring the empties back to my desk." So at Ralph's funeral, I saw Linda and gave her two of the cartridges.

I said, "Don't lose these, now."

I've got the other two at home — in case she loses those, I guess.

I went to Knox Junior High for seventh and eighth grades. I was part of the next-to-last freshman class at Boyden High School. I graduated from Boyden in 1968, and graduated from Catawba in 1972. I didn't know what I wanted to do.

High school memories

Kee Kirchin is one of my best friends. He's not Locke Long, Jr., but a neat guy and close friend. When we were 16, he had a Mustang and I had a Camaro. We had our first double date together. I was gonna drive, and he was working the parking lot at Belk-Harry at Christmastime in Downtown Salisbury. He took up the quarters and if the customer bought something, she'd get a receipt stamped and he'd give her the quarter back.

Kee said, "I've got to work until 6."

I said, "I will pick up the girls and bring them to your house while you take a shower and get ready."

The year was 1966, and we were taking the girls to see The Monkees at the Winston-Salem Coliseum. I was nervous. I went by and picked up the girls and took them to the Kirchins' house. When they got in the car, you couldn't put a dime between the girls' knees. We sat in the living room while Kee was getting ready. Not a word was said. You could cut the air with a knife.

Mrs. Kirchin walked into the living room, and behind her trotted their little Chihuahua mix, Sloopy.

Mrs. Kirchin said, "Would y'all like a Coca-Cola?"

I said, "No thanks, Mrs. Kirchin."

The two girls rolled their eyes.

Mrs. Kirchin walked out of the room. The Chihuahua walked around and smelled each of our feet.

The girls rolled their eyes.

And then, the little dog went to the center of the Persian rug, stuck up both hind legs, dragged its butt in a figure 8, and ran out of the room. It was awkward.

My mother had bought me a book by Ann Landers to get through the trials and tribulations of being a teenager. Somewhere around page 89, the book said, "Whenever you're in an awkward moment, think of something humorous to say."

I said, "Could y'all do that?"

What a horrible thing to say! But it sounded humorous at the time.

They rolled their eyes again.

Longest trip to Winston-Salem I've ever spent in my life.

Kee and I enjoyed the concert. Then we took 'em home. Never dated them again — by mutual agreement.

Chris Agner's mother, Martha, had a 1966 Mercury four-door Comet. But unlike most of our mothers' cars, this happened to have a 390-cubic inch engine. Chris Agner and several of us guys had just turned 16, and we took it down to the Farmington Drag Strip, unbeknownst to Mrs. Agner. Chris drove the car, and we sat in the stands. He won two races in that car and got two trophies. We absolutely loved it.

They put him up against cars like Chevrolet 396-cubic inch Chevelles. But since Chris had a family-type car, they put him two car lengths ahead of the GTO or the Chevelle he'd be running against. That was part of the rules of the drag strip association. He beat them. He had a half-car length at the end of the quarter-mile. It was fabulous.

We never told Mrs. Agner about it, other than the fact that we drove over to the drag strip and back in her car. Chris did keep the trophies and years later, when I became a patient of his, I asked if he still had the trophies. He said, "No. Of course, I remember the trip and winning the trophies, but I guess over the years, they just got gone."

What a shame.

Ironically, years later, when I turned 16, my mother prayed and said that she had raised me, and she was putting me in the Lord's hands for safekeeping.

So far, it's worked.

I met Chris Whisenant in kindergarten at First Presbyterian. He was a neat guy. I've got a picture of us. I'm sitting beside a picture of Jesus and Chris is on down the line a little bit. He looks like he's got mischief in his eye. We had so much fun playing together. We had a mutual love of cars, and later, girls. We stayed good friends over the years, and reconnected in high school. He worked for his dad at City Furniture and Appliance from the time he was 13 until his dad sold the business. He bought a 1964 Chevrolet Impala 409 with two four-barrel carburetors. Man, that car would move. It was red with a white interior, four-speed manual transmission. We drove that car everywhere.

We were 16, and we all tried to pitch in a dollar because it drank gas.

He also had an extremely rare 1966 Corvette with a 454-cubic inch engine in it. The engine was so big in that Corvette that when people would drive them a lot, they'd put a beer can on each side of the hood — the hood opened from the back — to create more air flow and keep the engine from overheating. So if you saw a Corvette cruising with two cans of beer in the back of the hood, you knew it had the 454 in it. Shortly before Chris died, I talked to him about buying that Corvette. He'd had enough fun with it. He reached in his pocket and pulled out the key and said, "Whenever you're ready."

But shortly after that, he died from cancer complications.

During high school, Chris worked for his dad, and for Brad Ragan after graduation. He went to a junior college for a semester, and as he told me, "I learned all I needed to learn." He worked himself up through the ranks with Brad and did extremely well out there.

About 15 years ago, maybe more, he moved down the street on Pine Tree Road. Every Saturday, he and Kent Roberts and Keith Garner and I got together. From 3 to 5, we got together and sipped on a beer or soft drink and talked about what we'd done over the past week. At 5, we broke up and went home.

Chris passed away several years after we'd all gotten back together. Chris was a lifelong smoker and got cancer of the throat. He went through tremendous radiation treatments, and I went down to his house a couple of times after he'd had a treatment. He'd be lying on his living room floor with a wet washcloth he wiped his face with. I just went over there and patted him on the back a little bit. I didn't say a word. He didn't feel like talking. He went through the whole program and everything was going well until his blood cell counts got off.

Eventually, I got a call that he was in ICU. I didn't think it was that big of a deal, but Kent and I went over. They let us in. I saw him lying in that bed and I knew it was the end. I really thought he was gonna be OK because he'd been through everything. For my good friend to die was beyond my comprehension.

His family then had to make the decision to take him off life support. His little brother, David, was holding his hand when he died a few minutes later. It was very, very sad. The indestructible Chris Whisenant had died. This was a fella who went on rooftops, installing roto antennas for his dad's company. Some people you just think are never gonna die. They've got a pass from death. It was just so sad.

The last several years of his life, Chris had been hell-bent for leather, so to speak. He never cared much for church, but he heard Kent, Keith and I talking about the Everyman's Bible Class.

He said, "Why don't y'all invite me to go?"

We looked at each other and were stunned.

"Hell, we've invited you a dozen times over the years."

"I'll be there this Sunday."

And he was there every single Sunday until he died. His wife would join him for the 11 o'clock church service. They were there every Sunday. They would go to every class that was put on by the church on any topic.

Earlier, in our hell-raising days, he came over to my college apartment and had a pint of Country Club Bourbon — now you know that's gonna be high class — and two sisters. So we put on a Steppenwolf album, cut the lights off, left the aquarium lights on, and sipped Country Club bourbon and watched the fish swim. That was a neat evening.

But on Pine Tree Road, we always had fun recalling the old days, hooting and hollering. For two hours every Saturday, middle-aged men became young boys once again.

My own struggle

My childhood was idyllic, but tragedy struck just shy of my 13th birthday.

I was diagnosed with ulcerative colitis. Up until that time, I was active in sports. I was a good baseball player. I played for the church all-star team. I played first base. I was active in public speaking. All that changed with my diagnosis in October 1963 and colostomy in November 1975. I think in my case, it was genetics in the McNeill side of the family. I still have some digestive issues. My parents did everything to try to find a cure for me.

They had an audio system installed at Boyden High School. The speaker at home was connected to my bed. At school, there was a small box with a handle on it and a plug. A classmate — usually Locke Long, Jr., — would carry this box from class to class, so I could hear and talk. It was two-way communication. It was pretty advanced for those days. Teachers would come by and help me in person. That's how I was able to keep up with my studies and not have to repeat a grade, which was very important.

We all figured there was a cure for ulcerative colitis back in 1963. Looking back, there wasn't. I spent Christmas 1963 in Rowan Memorial Hospital hooked up to IVs. And Christmas 1964 in Baptist Hospital hooked up to IVs.

Damn the bad luck! But I wasn't going to let it get to me. It wasn't going to defeat me. Yet I couldn't help but think how everything that was going so good could turn and suddenly go so bad.

When I did finally have surgery at age 25, it improved my quality of life. It's sort of like phantom pain. Since I had that illness for 10 years in my formative years, it had an effect on my life. I like to look at it as the old Nietzsche saying: "That which doesn't kill us makes us stronger."

Dr. Lynch Murphy was my doctor, and he said I'd be looking at colon cancer if we didn't go ahead and do something. I couldn't have been more pleased with how things turned out. I was married to a wonderful, understanding wife, and we are still married today. It was tough. I've been aggressive all my life — somewhat driven when it comes to business. It's been like that all my life. It put some roadblocks up there. I could have been a stronger employee, a stronger executive, if my body from the neck down could have equaled what it is from the neck up.

I could have been more successful — but at what cost, I don't know. Looking back now, I'm happy. Over the years, whenever I had some tough spots I said, "Well, you could be on Saipan, firing a machine gun, waiting on the Marines." That puts it in pretty good perspective.

My best friend, Locke Long, Jr., made me feel really good when he said this recently: "Hap has been hugely successful. What else could he have done? He could have ruled the world. I never thought of him as being held back at all because of his illness."

I had decided to go to Catawba College, a liberal arts school. I did not take physics or chemistry in high school. I took drafting at Boyden and won first place in the state for mechanical drafting, level 3, the highest level.

I signed up for chemistry under Dr. Wendell Detty and I made an A in it and I liked it. I thought I might major in chemistry. But as a sophomore, I had to take intermediate French or German as part of my degree requirement. I did not do well in French at Boyden, and I chose not to take German at Catawba.

So I changed over to business, which included accounting classes. I figured, why not just major in accounting? I thought it would help me more than a business degree. That got me in the door with Sherrill and Smith, which at the time was the CPA firm for a small company called Food Town. My senior year in college, Sherrill and Smith hired me as a junior accountant. I started work in August before my senior year, with the contingency that if I did well, they would hire me full-time. And that's what happened.

My first three years of Catawba, I had worked 40 to 50 hours a week at Towne Pharmacy. During each of those years, I took a full class load of 15 hours a semester. I got out of classes about 11 or 11:30 a.m., and I would go straight to my apartment and do my homework. I grabbed a bite and would be at Towne Pharmacy at 1 p.m and work 'til 9 p.m. Then, if there was any other homework I needed to do, I'd do it when I got off at 9. I worked every other weekend, which was 9 a.m.-9 p.m. on Saturday and 1-9 p.m. on Sunday.

I did a little bit of everything there. I started out sweeping the parking lot. Then I moved inside and swept and mopped the floors. We did that every night. I did deliveries. I helped at the soda fountain. I helped on the cash registers. I answered the phones when needed. I would pull prescriptions out for refills. Fred Medlin owned

Towne Pharmacy and would hire kids from high school part-time. I started with him my senior year in high school cleaning the parking lot and continued through my junior year in college.

I'd be in bed by 11 o'clock every night and I had my own apartment, so there was no partying. Every other weekend I was off, so that was social time.

Back in 1971, I got tickets to see The Who in concert while their drummer, Keith Moon, was still alive. I worked long hours at Towne Pharmacy, but it afforded me the opportunity to go to concerts and do different things.

I bought the tickets, and then, about two weeks before the concert, my date, who played field hockey, broke her leg.

I said, "Don't worry, I can sell the tickets."

She said, "Like hell you're selling the tickets. The Who doesn't come around often. We're going!"

I had a 240-Z. We got her crutches and I piled her into the car and we went down there. Two guys from Spartanburg helped me get her to our seats and back to the car. She was not to be denied seeing Keith Moon and The Who.

In 1971, I took Trina Hall to see Steppenwolf Live at the Park Center in Charlotte. It was a fabulous concert. We had a huge time down there. It was at the time the band, whose lead singer was John Kay, came out with the Steppenwolf Live album. Everybody was hooting and hollering and we put our dates on our shoulders. They ended up with three of their most popular songs, "The Pusher," "Magic Carpet," and "Born to Be Wild." Everybody went absolutely crazy when they played those three songs.

Concert list
1966-1992

- The Monkees — Winston-Salem Coliseum, Winston-Salem, NC, Dec. 29, 1966
- The Tams — The Crystal Lounge, Catawba College, Salisbury, NC, 1967
- The Brooklyn Bridge — Keppel Auditorium, Catawba College, Salisbury, NC, 1969
- Sha Na Na — Keppel Auditorium, Catawba College, Salisbury, NC, 1969
- Steppenwolf — The Park Center, Charlotte, NC, June 5, 1970
- Three Dog Night — Charlotte Coliseum, Charlotte, NC, 1970
- The Rolling Stones — Charlotte Coliseum, Charlotte, NC, 1970, 1973
- Sly and the Family Stone — Keppel Auditorium, Catawba College, Salisbury, NC,

1971
- Emerson, Lake and Palmer — Charlotte Coliseum, Charlotte, NC, 1971
- Deep Purple — Charlotte Coliseum, Charlotte, NC, 1971
- The Who — Charlotte Coliseum, Charlotte, NC, Nov. 20, 1971
- Peter Frampton — Greensboro Coliseum, Greensboro, NC, 1976
- The Marshall Tucker Band — Greensboro Coliseum, Greensboro, NC, 1976
- Eric Clapton — Charlotte Coliseum, Charlotte, NC, March 30, 1990; 1993
- New Kids on the Block — Groves Stadium, Winston-Salem, NC, Aug. 15, 1990
- Tom Petty and The Heartbreakers — Blockbuster Pavilion, Charlotte, NC, Oct. 15, 1991
- Van Halen — Charlotte Coliseum, Charlotte, NC, Feb. 28, 1992
- Eric Clapton with Roger Forrester — Charlotte Coliseum, Charlotte, NC, May 2, 1992
- Ringo Starr — Blockbuster Pavilion, Charlotte, NC, June 6, 1992
- Lollapalooza II — Blockbuster Pavilion, Charlotte, NC, Aug. 25, 1992
- Michael Bolton — Blockbuster Pavilion, Charlotte, NC, Aug. 7, 1992

Parking lot research

I was always insecure about money. The cotton business was up or down. H.K. Roberts and Sons was flush or not. Fortunately, they made more than they lost at the end of the day, but not the secure money I had seen the first five or 10 years of my life. Being the obsessive-compulsive type I am, I became insecure about money. So I wanted money.

At Towne Pharmacy, they started me out at about a dollar an hour. When I left I was making $2.25 an hour. It put gas in my car and got me some good dates. I got tickets to some great concerts in Charlotte. I saw the Rolling Stones at the old Charlotte Coliseum, Steppenwolf Live at the Park Center in Charlotte, Eric Clapton, Earth, Wind & Fire, The Who twice, Deep Purple, Three Dog Night ... I even thought about going to Woodstock. Thank God that didn't happen. I probably wouldn't have gotten back.

I didn't have to spend a lot of time studying. I went to class and took notes. Accounting started to click with me. OK, I thought, I got this. I understand this. I like this.

When I did deliveries at Towne Pharmacy, I would look at a paint store and think, I wonder how they do their accounting. Theory became practice and vice versa. Oddly enough, that's how I scoped out

Food Town. We had a good trade at Towne Pharmacy. I took deliveries out all over town. It was free. I never got a tip. Never, not once. I'm a good tipper today. I noticed Food Towns had very few cars in the parking lot, and I wondered, "How do they stay in business?"

Then Mr. Ketner came out with the famous concept of Lowest Food Prices in North Carolina (LFPINC), and I noticed the parking lots start filling up with cars. When it started catching on, I could see all four Food Towns in Salisbury growing by the number of cars in the parking lot. That piqued my interest. I took $1,000 of the money I saved working at Towne Pharmacy and bought 50 shares of Food Town stock on July 6, 1971.

Before long, I saw my stock split, 2 for 1, and I had 100 shares. I developed an instant love for Food Town.

I had done my parking lot research, and I was ready for the next chapter in my life.

1941: Hap McNeill.

Left — 1942: Hap's namesake, John Charles McNeill, was his mother's brother. He signed up for the Army after Pearl Harbor. He was killed on Saipan on July 4, 1944.

Below — 1942: Another photo of Hap.

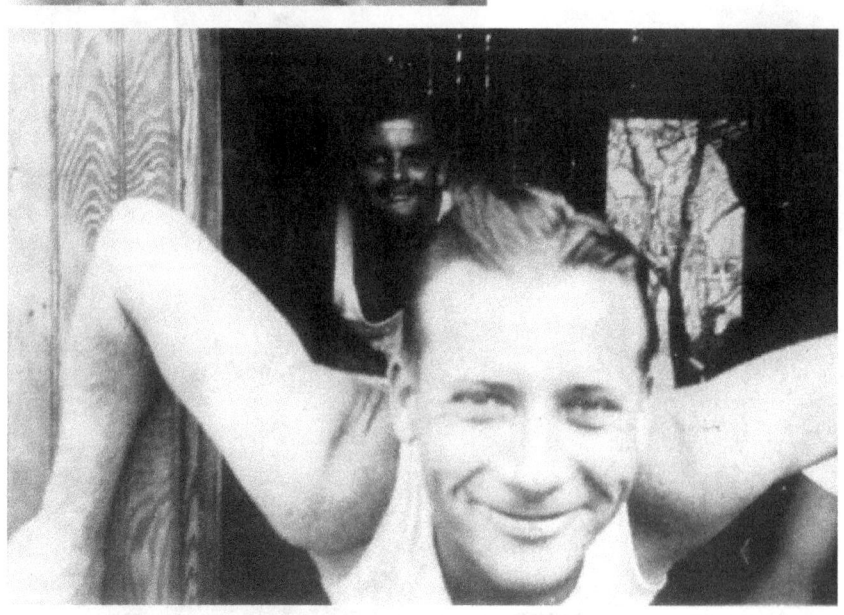

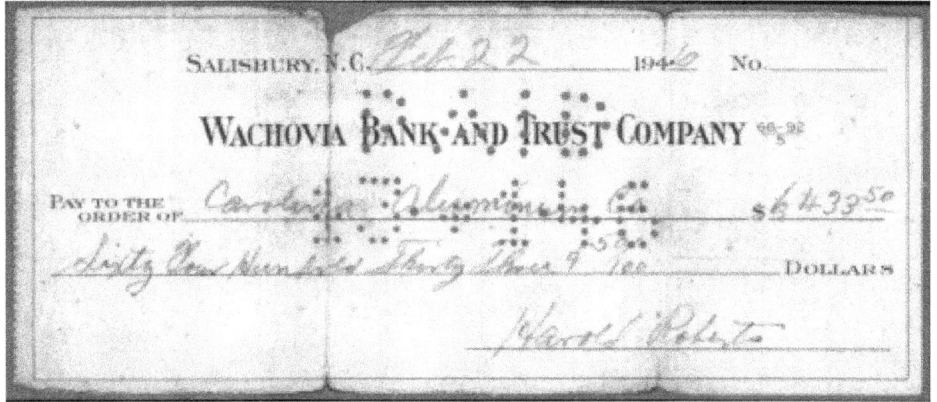

Top left — 1968: Locke Long, Jr. and Hap won a state drafting award. Locke went on to become an engineer while Hap founded his own CPA firm and later Statewide Title.

Top right — 1950: A tile with Hap's name, birth date and birth time.

Middle — 1946: The check Hap's dad wrote to purchase their family farm.

Below left — 1950s: Photo of Hap's dad's vehicle being shipped to Salisbury. H.K. Roberts always drove Pontiacs with large engines.

Below right — 1950s: Hap on his horse, Tony, with his dog, Rusty, at the family farm.

Bottom — 1950s: Doo-Doo Raynor and Hap, who is holding a large, dead copperhead snake.

Above — 1954: Hap in preschool at First Presbyterian Church with Angie Barker, standing, the girl who stuck the bead up her nose.

Below — The micro midget, which Hap received for Christmas 1956.

1962: Marilyn Monroe's funeral bulletin. Ralph Roberts was one of only about 30 people who were invited to attend by Joe DiMaggio.

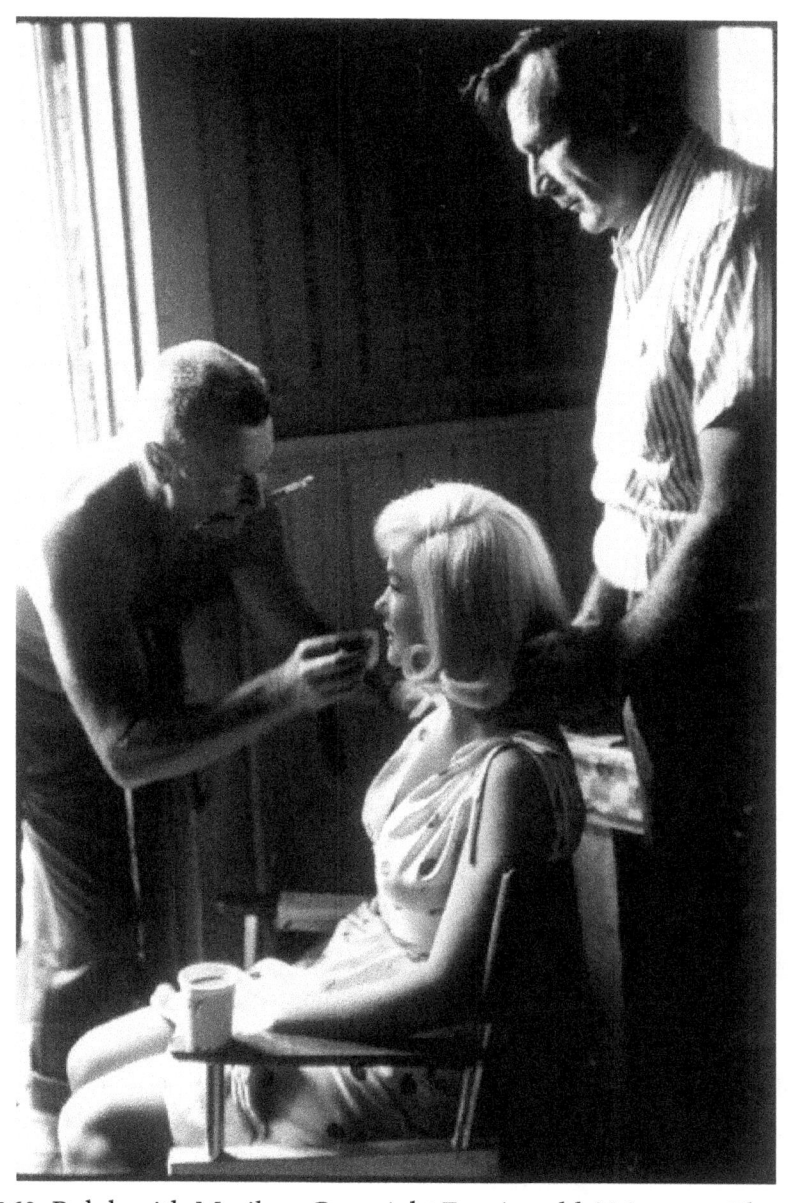

1960: Ralph with Marilyn. Copyright Eve Arnold / Magnum Photos

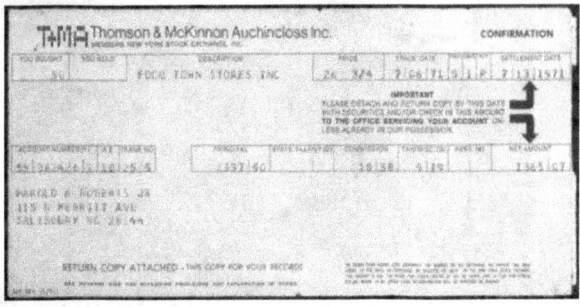

Above left — 1977: A ticket stub from the 1977 World Series. The Yankees won in a thrilling game 6 against the Dodgers with three home runs from Reggie Jackson, and Hap was there.

Above right — 1963: Hap with his parents, H.K. and Idell Roberts, shortly after he was diagnosed with ulcerative colitis.

Middle — 1971: Hap purchased his first Food Town stock on July 6, 1971, a few months before going to work full-time for the company.

Left — Undated head shot of Ralph Roberts, the uncle everyone always wanted to have.

1982: A portrait of Hap, Annette, and Heather the year Hap retired from Food Town.

Above — 2019: Hap's 1982 280ZX Turbo, the present he gave himself when he left Food Town Stores, Inc.

Below — Larry Raley, Hap, and Allyn Adams, all of Food Town, with Kimberly Tomes, Miss USA 1977, who was in town for a parade. Food Town sponsored the dinner afterward.

Above left — 1969: Annette.

Above right — 1983: Hap in London.

Right — 2001: Annette.

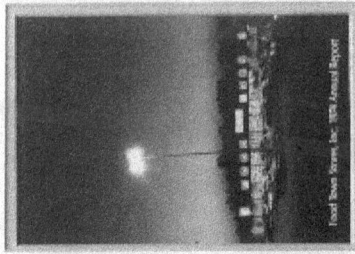

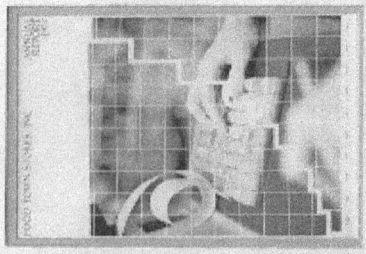

Left — The first public annual reports at Food Town, from 1970 to 1979. Below — Annual reports of Ryan's Steakhouses during the first five years of the company, when Hap served on its board of directors.

Left — 1983: Heather, on her 6th birthday, with her dad on a trip to New York City.

Right — 1995: Photo of Hap at home in a white dinner jacket.

Board of Directors. Standing from left to right: Jack P. Tate, Barry L. Edwards, James M. Shoemaker, Jr., Harold K. Roberts, Jr. Seated from left to right: Alvin A. McCall, Jr., Charles D. Way. Vernon L. Hamm not pictured.

Mid-1980s: Photo of Ryan's Steakhouse board. Standing from left to right: Jack P. Tate, Barry L. Edwards, James M. Shoemaker, Jr., Harold K. Roberts, Jr. Seated from left to right: Alvin A. McCall, Jr., Charles D. Way.

Above left — 1995: Hap at the Heart Ball with Jayne Helms, Ann Ellis and Annette.

Above right — 2011: Hap and Annette before the Heart Ball, which they attended and supported for many years.

Right — 1989: Hap and Alvin McCall at the grand opening of Ryan's Steakhouse in Kannapolis.

Top Row L-R
Hap Roberts
Beau Taylor
Clifford Ray
Donnie Marsh
Jim Berrier
Ronnie Marsh

Bottom Row L-R
Wilson L. Smith
Tommy Eller
Ronnie Smith
Last Outing for Cliff Ray
Tommy Eller's House
January, 1990

January 1990: The Food Town "mavericks" visit with Clifford Ray shortly before his death. Top Row L-R: Hap Roberts, Beau Taylor, Clifford Ray, Donnie Marsh, Jim Berrier, Ronnie Marsh. Bottom Row L-R: Wilson L. Smith, Tommy Eller, Ronnie Smith.

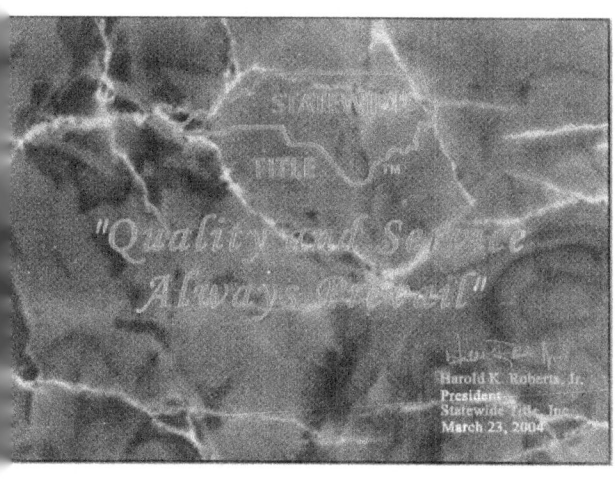

Above — 1991: Meredith Lassiter Brincefield and Heather Roberts Brady behind the Statewide Title sign.

Left — Statewide Title motto "Quality and Service Always Prevail"®

Above and below — Christmas 1994: Ralph Roberts, Hap's mother Idell Roberts, Hap Roberts and Heather Roberts.

Above — 1993: Hap and Annette took Heather to New York City for her 16th birthday. They stayed at The Plaza hotel.

Below — 2000: Hap at his 50th birthday at the Country Club of Salisbury. All the guests were ladies, and the group dined on filet mignon and champagne.

Far left — Hap with Heather after learning she was going to be a debutante for the 1996 Terpsichorean Ball in Raleigh.

Middle right — 1993: Heather and Hap on a trip to New York City for her 16th birthday.

Below right — 2007: Heather and Hap on a trip to New York City for her 30th birthday.

Bottom — 1994: Annette, Heather and Hap in the snow.

Above — 2013: From left, Annette's parents, L.P. and Joyce Barker Bell, with Heather, Annette and Bell. Mrs. Bell died Nov. 27, 2018.

Below — 2013: Brad Brady, Heather's husband; L.P. and Joyce Bell, Heather with Bell, and Annette and Hap.

Above — 2013: Ralph Ketner and Hap. Ketner proved a demanding boss, but in later years told Hap what a good job he'd done while at Food Town.

Below — 2019: Crunch time. Getting the book ready for print. Clockwise from left, Hap Roberts, Wanda Peffer, Steve Jacobs, Annette Roberts, Sarah Michalec, Susan Shinn Turner, and Chris Preslar.

2016: Annette, Heather, Brad, and Hap pose around Graham and Bell.

2015: Hap and Annette with their dogs, Greta, Ava and Lilli.

Part II: The Food Town years 1972-1982 and beyond

1995: Head shot of Hap.

Food Town

I went to work for Sherrill and Smith full-time in June 1972. Two months later, one of the senior accountants there said that Jim Berrier, the corporate secretary at Food Town, wanted to know something. I remember the senior accountant telling me, "Sherrill would kill me if he knew I was telling you this, but Jim Berrier wants to know if you'd be interested in going to work for Food Town."

I said, "Why not? Let's give it a try."

I was 21 years old. They had 10 or 12 stores then. They put me to work and they threw it at me.

I was assistant controller. There was no controller. Jim Berrier was secretary and office manager, and Ralph Ketner was president and treasurer. Between Berrier and Ketner, they handled the accounting.

Now, you tell me the pressure of a 21-year-old working for a 52-year-old mathematical genius. That's pressure. That did not help my ulcerative colitis. But he whipped me into shape.

On the other hand, it was extremely exciting working with these mavericks. Most of them had worked for Glenn Ketner, Sr., and some of them worked with Winn-Dixie. We learned a lot from these mavericks. They knew the business, and they all had a good sense of humor. There was a "buy New York, sell Chicago" atmosphere that prevailed.

For example, when we moved over to Harrison Road, we turned our old warehouse on Julian Road into a refrigerated warehouse. Clifford Ray was over there with the warehouse people and did his buying over there. Jim Berrier and I would ride over occasionally to check in with Cliff. We had rotary dial phones back then, and Ralph's number was 21. Every time we would go over to see Cliff, he would kid us, saying, "What are y'all doing over here? You need to be over on Harrison Road. Let me call the man." He'd dial "2" and then "1" and he'd hang up before the "1" went through. One time his finger slipped and he hung up real quick. He'd heard, "All right!" which was how Mr. Ketner answered the phone.

But they were all just really neat people, with good common sense. All of them worked well with their people. It was really a lot of fun, working and learning from them. As the company got bigger, they started retiring. We started getting the MBAs in there, and it was a totally different atmosphere. It wasn't as much fun working alongside them as it was The Mavericks.

Our corporate office was over the warehouse on

Julian Road. We were next to Jim Berrier and two doors down from Mr. Ketner. Wilson Smith was out on the road most of the time at the stores as he was head of operations. We didn't have any extra chairs in the offices. If someone came to see you, they talked in front of your desk and then went back to what they were doing. But if we had to meet, I'd give Jim Berrier or Mr. Ketner my chair, and I'd sit on the edge of the big, gray trashcan. It was about the size of a chair. When we had our offices on top of the warehouse in Julian Road, we'd have visits from all these New York analysts and stockbrokers.

They were just appalled at us having linoleum floors, and old furniture from the Ketner Supermarket days. The way our stock was performing, they expected to come down and see lavish carpet, side chairs, and sofas, and all that get up. They didn't realize you don't make money off carpet, sofas and side chairs. You make money by working, watching every nickel, and putting it into inventory, not sofas. Inventory you can resell. You put that extra material in the warehouse, not spend money so somebody can prop up on a sofa.

When we got into the new offices, I had my desk and my swivel chair. They wanted me to start talking to the New York bankers and analysts and brokers. I asked Jim Berrier if I could go ahead and get two chairs to use in front of my desk. He said, "What do you need them for?" I said, "When I'm talking to the people from New York, I'm not gonna ask them to prop on the edge of a trashcan like I've done." He laughed and said, "OK."

Food Town had opened in 1957. I was there at the first store. Aunt Mabel's two daughters were at Catawba College. They held my hand, and the three of us walked up there to the opening. I got a helium balloon and a free Coke.

All the head guys were mavericks: Clifford Ray, Wilson Smith, Jim Berrier, Tommy Eller, the Marsh twins, Beau Taylor, O.L. Casey. Just a great group of mavericks — no MBAs, a few college degrees. But mainly, they learned under Glenn Ketner, Sr. of Ketner Supermarkets. They all had worked for him.

Glenn Sr. sold out to Winn-Dixie, and some of those guys went to work for Winn-Dixie in Raleigh. About a year later, Glenn Ketner, Sr. built Ketner Center and planned to have a grocery store as the anchor tenant. Glenn Sr. signed a non-compete covenant so he couldn't own stock in the new company.

So Ralph Ketner, Brown Ketner and Wilson Smith started Food Town. Jim Berrier stayed on and worked with Glenn Sr. for two years. Then Jim joined Food Town about 1959.

I did my best to soak it all up. It was somewhat overwhelming. Ralph was just so smart. He did all of his working papers in ink. That means you have to be pretty accurate. He taught me to be more obsessive and compulsive in that regard. He was tough and demanding. He always said he was no harder on anyone than he was on himself. He was extremely hard on me because accounting and numbers were his forte. I was right there in the middle of his domain. But I hung in there, and I had his blessings there toward the end. But it was too late for me. I was burned out. Time for an MBA to take my place.

Tom Smith worked with Hap during Hap's tenure at Food Town. Smith started with the company as a bag boy and later became its CEO. He retired from Food Lion in 1999. Here are his thoughts about Hap:

I came back to Food Town in 1970 from Del Monte and Hap started in 1972. He worked with Jim Berrier. I wasn't too involved in accounting. I remember the day he introduced Annette to us. I could hear them coming!

Hap was a pleasant guy to work with. Whatever you asked for, he'd try to get it. Something about Christmas always turned Hap on. He'd always go through the office, wishing everyone a Merry Christmas.

We had sort of a unique situation at Food Town. Everybody was involved. People worked hard and Hap was one of them. We all put in way more than normal hours. But Hap always kept that smile on his face. We never knew from day to day what was going to be coming up, but we were accomplishing things, and a lot was happening.

In 1970, we had 12 stores. When we started growing, we added several hundred stores, and we couldn't help but be proud of seeing the company grow. We had lower prices statewide than Big Star or A&P. We were taking pride in what we were doing, and we had excellent employee benefits, too.

As things grew, we had to get different people with different talents. Because of the stock growing so much, those who left were set to go into another business or retire. I never had complaints on Hap as far as his work or how he got along with people. He had a great approach with people.

Shortly after Hap joined Food Town in 1972, he got a taste of life in the fast lane. He recounted the following story to Mark Wineka in the book "Lion's Share."

Soon after his joining the company in August 1972, Food Town had its secondary stock offering in October. Ralph Ketner was supposed to assemble some paperwork and attend a meeting one day with the underwriters in Pittsburgh. But he had another commitment…

"OK, this is what we got to do," Ketner told Roberts when he got to the president's office that morning. "You're supposed to be in Pittsburgh this afternoon to deliver some documents. The documents need to be signed by Bill Sherrill of Sherrill and Smith. Then they need to be taken over to the CPA firm in Asheboro. They need to be signed. Then they need to be taken to Washburn Press in Charlotte. And so, you'll get a final brief from Washburn Press, get on a 4 o'clock plane, and they'll wait for you at Parker/Hunter. You haven't got time to go home and pack or do anything. Just make a couple of calls and tell them you won't be home tonight. If you are, it'll be late."

Roberts was off. He easily gathered the signatures of Bill Sherrill in Salisbury, but he ran into problems in Asheboro, about an hour's drive away. The Asheboro accountant's father had become ill and was in the local hospital. He refused to see Roberts, who made a desperate call to Ketner.

"Oh, my God, plead with him like a Dutch uncle," Ketner said. But the accountant refused to see Roberts or the papers. He wanted to stay with his sick father. Roberts called back, and Ketner was able to reschedule the Pittsburgh meeting for 3 o'clock the next afternoon.

"You've got to have the documents signed," he ordered. "You've got to have everything ready."

Roberts checked into an Asheboro motel, but continued his efforts to talk with the accountant. "I gave an orderly in the hospital $10 to ask him if he would come and see me," Roberts recalls. "That made him mad. So I just waited, and he said, 'I'll be in my office at 9 o'clock in the morning.'" Roberts was able to talk him into an 8 a.m. meeting.

He went to a nearby drugstore for a toothbrush and toothpaste, and spent the night in Asheboro. The next morning, he put on the same clothes from the day before and rushed to the Asheboro office for the signatures. Finally, success.

Roberts started on his two-hour drive toward Charlotte. As his Datsun 240-Z hurtled down a country back road at about 75 mph, he realized that he had to go to the bathroom. Fearing he would lose precious minutes by stopping, Roberts reached for a paper cup on the floorboard. He used it as a portable urinal and slowed the car enough to dump the contents out the window. He kept the cup, thinking he might need it again. Roberts made it to Washburn Press and his flight out of Charlotte.

In Pittsburgh, he met the men from Parker/Hunter, handed over the documents, and, dragging from nervous exhaustion, turned an about-face for the trip home.

"And that," Roberts says of the hectic days with Food Town, "was par for the course."

***

My stomach is hurting now just thinking about this. But I knew we had a winner. I knew I could handle it for 10 years, then let the cards fall where they may. I got a stock option early on during the worst recession of the 1970s. Then the recession ended. The Belgians bought one-third of our stock in 1974, but the stock options were not exercisable at that time. In 1976, the Belgians bought controlling interest, 51 percent. The stock was not exercisable then either. That same year, I was made controller.

I exercised my stock option on Friday, Oct. 13, 1978. It was exercisable then. I bought my house at 21 Pine Tree Road on that day. I had some cash and then I borrowed the rest of the money from Gary Taylor at Northwestern Bank.

In 1977, Ralph wanted me to visit a company called Shop-Rite in Elizabeth, N.J. About that time, the Yankees were in the World Series. I worked it out so I could go to a Yankees game. I had a rental car, so I drove it from Elizabeth to the Bronx. I got there about 3 p.m. so I could see the players coming in. Reggie Jackson drove up in a burgundy Rolls Royce convertible. I went in and got my seat, got a hot dog and got a beer. That was the night Reggie hit three home runs. The Yankees won the World Series. Everybody was going crazy. I went out on the field.

Later on, I got to my car. Then I got to thinking, how in the hell am I gonna get out of here and get across the George Washington Bridge? I was in a 1977 Plymouth Belvedere, four-door.

I saw a nicely dressed man on the street and said, "Hey buddy, can you tell me how to get across the bridge?" He said, "I'll tell you if you give me a lift. I need to get across the George Washington Bridge, because I can call a cab from there and it'll be a lot cheaper." I said, "You got a deal."

He told me how to get out of there and get across the bridge. He was a bond salesman for Salomon Brothers. I got back to Elizabeth, N.J., safe and sound. I went to the bar and had a drink and looked at the news following the game. Billy Martin was the manager then. The Yankees won the series that year. That was a good time.

I had bought other stock and it had split 3-for-1

three times. By 1982, I was in a position to retire. I didn't sell all my stock, but I had some cash and I had some other investments. My health was starting to suffer, so it was time. I retired from Food Town at age 31. I didn't know what I was going to do, but I knew I had to do something. I left at the right time. I am not stubborn.

Fortunately, that's the way it turned out. I left at the right time, I took time off with Annette and Heather, and started new ventures, thanks to the financial trappings of Food Town Stores, Inc., and the mavericks who built it. Hopefully, I had a small part of helping them do it.

Here's how Mark Wineka chronicled Hap's exit from Food Town in Lion's Share:

Hap Roberts, a homegrown product, learned about the fast track early. He stayed with the company from 1972 to 1982, joining as a 21-year-old and retiring for health reasons at 31. As assistant controller and, later, controller, Roberts' duties at such a young age were considerable: He handled banking relationships and cash management, compliance with the Securities and Exchange Commission, investment policies, four-week income statements, shareholder relations, internal audits, acquisition and conversion of stores from competitors, inventory control, the company policy manual, weekly financial data transmittal, risk management, cash-flow projections, modified accounting systems and more.

"I just didn't want to maintain the pace that I had maintained," Roberts says. "At Food Lion, you go up or you go out. That's as simple as it is. I would have lost my family, I'm sure, if I would have stayed. I mean there were some times we would work 40 and 50 days straight when we were buying stores from competitors. My normal work week was 60 hours, and I would be there at quarter 'til eight and leave there at quarter of seven Monday through Friday, and Saturday I would work from nine to about one-thirty, quarter of two."

Roberts knew within a couple of weeks of joining Food Lion, then Food Town, that the environment wasn't his cup of tea, but he was hard-headed and young enough to want to prove himself. The stock options he took were also golden handcuffs. As a child, Roberts had ulcerative colitis and the residuals from that — complicated by job pressures — put him in the hospital three times during his last year with Food Town. He eventually had surgery that left him weak and susceptible to illness. He stayed run down. When he became ill, he risked dehydration. He would go to the hospital for intravenous fluids. "I knew I couldn't keep on going like that and keep my family, my health and sanity," he says.

When he left Food Town, Roberts felt like he had lost a spouse. He loved and respected the men who built the company: Ketner, Smith, Tommy Eller, Jim Berrier and Clifford Ray. "Mavericks built Food Lion," he says. "I don't know who's maintaining it now, but it was built by mavericks. They spoiled me. I loved them. I guess you get spoiled once you've been exposed and get a taste of that side of the organization."

Buying mom and pop operations

When I was at Food Town, I was in charge of buying stores we'd buy from mom-and-pop operations. Ketner would work out what we'd pay for equipment. The sellers would have an independent inventory crew, and we'd have an independent inventory crew. We'd draw up sheets, and I'd have someone merge the data. Gary Morgan, Dewey Preslar, Duane Wilson, and Gary Cauble were with me. They would go through the store, making sure there were no out-of-date items before the inventory crew got there. Any major discrepancies, we'd have the aisles recounted by both crews.

We had a locksmith come and change locks and change the safe combination, or if the safe was old, we'd have a new safe brought in. One of the guys would meet with the NCR rep to make sure registers were right. If they weren't NCRs we'd swap them out. I'd have one man on the front door and one man on the back, and nobody went in or out so nothing would get gone. One time we did three stores in one day. They were big. We started early, but we got it done.

The point in saying all this is that we'd work 'til 1 p.m. on Saturday. Then we got into the swing of buying independent stores. We'd work about 40 days straight. We'd meet at headquarters at 3 p.m. Saturday, go to the location, have dinner, check into the hotel and watch TV. Then we'd usually meet the sellers of the store and their people at 7 on Sunday mornings. We always bought stores on Sunday. Usually it involved more than one store. One time, we bought six stores. Gary Morgan and his inventory crew were at three stores, then I was at the other three with my inventory crew.

Ever-Glo Sign Co. would do the sign changeover on Monday, Tuesday or Wednesday. That was operations, not what we were in charge of. We had it down to a fine art. We could do it pretty quickly. We did have some arguments about out-of-date merchandise. Back in those days, it was not printed legibly — it was all in code. One seller said, "It doesn't say anything about buying out-of-date merchandise." I said, "We are not doing that." The only instructions I had from Ralph were on one steno page. All your inventories are taken at retail and then you reduce it whatever amount you agree to. We got pretty good at it, and we got some pretty good stores, too — some we bought from Harris Teeter, believe it or not, that we bought in South Carolina and Georgia as we started expanding the circle. Most were mom-and-pop operations, but we did buy a few big stores. We had a small crew, we were lean and mean, and we knew what we were doing.

One other thing I developed before I left was a formal system of internal control for the distribution centers, the stores, and headquarters. It was about 100 pages, and I still have a copy. That was used for years after I left.

Hap recalled this period of buying existing stores to Mark Wineka in Lion's Share.

"All in all, during my time, we bought six stores from Oren Heffner, seven stores up in Tidewater, Virginia, we bought a store in Buena Vista, Virginia. We probably bought six Harris Teeter stores. We bought four or five Food Worlds. We bought four or five Lowe's Food Stores. We bought another 10 stores, you know, just scattered around, like two Giant Genie stores in Charlotte, a store in Eden from a private family. We just let them close down, and we went into them. No. 64 in Statesville was an old A&P…"

"One of the best stores we bought was No. 40

in Cary that we bought from Kroger. They must have had somebody sitting at a desk looking at printouts in Cincinnati, Ohio, who said that store's not making money. We bought it and within two months, it became our number one store."

***

In May 1974, Ralph got a call from Kroger that they had a store over in Cary that was not doing too well, and wanted to know if we were interested in buying it.

Ralph would give me a steno sheet of instructions for each conversion. He handled the equipment sale. Groceries were gross less 20 percent. Meat at cost. Produce at cost. A meat man would do the meat inventory. Clifford Ray would have a man do the produce. I had our inventory crew, they had their crew.

Annette and I had been married one month, and this store came up pretty quickly.

Ralph said, "Can you handle this on your own if you have your inventory crew?"

I said, "I'll take Annette with me. We'll go on a Saturday, check into a motel and be there at 7 a.m. Sunday when the crew comes."

First thing we did was have the locks changed and give the key to Annette.

"Don't let anybody in or out unless you call me," I told her.

The conversion went well. The only argument we had was over out-of-date merchandise in the grocery store.

It was just Annette and me there from Food Town. Kroger had 12 guys there. We agreed on a price. We all signed the documents at the end of the day.

One interesting thing I learned early on was all meat managers owned their own knives. Ralph told me, "Nothing leaves that store."

This meat manager was pissed off because he'd just lost his job. A unionized store had been sold to non-unionized Food Town.

Annette called me on the intercom to come to the front to tell me the meat man was about to leave the store with his knives. I went up and said, "You can't take those knives with you."

He pulled one out and pointed it at me and said, "These are my knives."

And I said, "OK, no problem."

I wasn't going to get killed over some knives.

The Mavericks

Jim Berrier was a kingpin, one of the unsung heroes of Food Town Stores, Inc.

He had served in WWII in Belgium, in the infantry. He went to Europe on a boat. He remembered the captain of the ship saying, "Do not go up to the top of this ship. If you're swept off the top of this ship, we cannot get you."

There were some boys from New York who wanted some fresh air. They opened the portholes, got on top of the boat, and were swept overboard. Goodbye, New York, New York.

Mr. Berrier said it was difficult going across the ocean in a boat, because there was water in the boat wherever you went. You were up to your mid-thighs. People got seasick, and that was floating around in the water. So it was not a pleasant journey across the ocean.

They were sent to Belgium and put on the line at night, and told to fire toward Germany, or a German-occupied area, which was most of Belgium.

I asked him, "Did you ever kill anybody?"

He said, "I have no idea. We were just told to lie down at night and shoot toward the occupied area." His brother was killed in Belgium, but Mr. Jim Berrier made it back.

He went on to graduate from Catawba in the late '40s, probably. He went to work for Glenn Ketner, Sr. in his supermarkets, and became his right-hand man in the office.

Ralph was a buyer for Glenn when he got out of the Army. Tommy Eller joined Ketner's toward the end of the war. Brown Ketner was the head meat man. Clifford Ray in produce. Wilson Smith in advertising and operations.

Ralph inherited a wonderful group of men.

They all went to Winn-Dixie in Raleigh, except for Jim Berrier. He stayed with Glenn Sr., who opened Ketner Center. He had a hardware store where Windsor Gallery is now. I remember going there and buying model airplanes.

Jim did the accounting for Food Town Stores, Inc., gratis, just to help them out. Jim worked for Glenn Sr. but headed up the accounting for the struggling, young Food Town Stores, Inc. He went full-time with Food Town as office manager in 1959, and was responsible for store audits, banking, accounting, personnel, insurance, and anything else they needed.

Truly, Jim Berrier was one of the unsung heroes. He and Mr. Ketner were both stubborn and hard-headed. He retired in 1982. He called me and said, "I went in and talked to Ralph, and Ralph said, 'You need to go ahead and retire.'"

I said, "If you're going, I'm going."

Tommy Eller also left. Wilson Smith and Clifford Ray had exited a couple of years earlier.

We were the last two of the mavericks to leave. We had a flood of MBAs who were coming in who thought they knew more than we did. It was a great time to go. Anytime you go out on top, it's good.

Jim was a great guy. He was like my big brother. So when he retired, I wanted to go with him. It was the end of the road for us.

Wilson Smith and I shared an office above the warehouse on Julian Road when I was first hired in 1972. He was a great guy — a good Christian, a good family man. He knew every single facet of operations in a grocery store. He was awfully good to me. He would tell me things only he and Jim Berrier would tell me. He liked me, and I liked him. He went on several store audits with me, and told me I was doing a good job.

I had a Datsun 240-Z. I never had a company car. Wilson Smith loved getting in that car with me and zipping in and out of traffic.

"We got over to Kernersville quickly!" he told Jim Berrier once.

Wilson had a tough life. His parents divorced when he was little. He used to deliver groceries in a wagon.

He served honorably in WWII. He came to work as advertising manager for Glenn Ketner, Sr. at Ketner's Supermarket. He moved into operations and went with them to Raleigh when they sold out to Winn-Dixie, then returned as one of the founders of Food Town Stores, Inc.

Ronnie Smith, Wilson's son, is a great guy. He was the first personnel manager we had. He was empathetic toward all employees. He knew what all the benefits were. Not only was he knowledgeable, but quite caring. He was not your typical legacy. He earned his space in the company.

He was a pilot in Vietnam. He could have gone to work for any of the commercial airlines as a pilot, but he chose to come back to his beloved company, Food Town.

To this day, I consider him a good friend.

Ronnie and Donnie Marsh were great guys. Their dad, Bill, and my dad were good friends — good hunting, fishing, and poker playing friends, along with Dr. F.O. Glover, Dr. Frazier, Dr. Walter Choate, and Bill Musselman. They played cards together, went hunting and fishing together, took semi-annual trips to Currituck Sound to fish. They were the predecessors to the group I went with. Their dad taught them how to hunt and fish, and they are the best in this county. It's got to be born in you. You've got to love it and have a passion for it — which I never did, but they did. They could teach you more sitting out in the cornfield than you could ever get by paying a professional guide. They just knew it. They had it in their blood, and they were capable of teaching it.

Their daddy died a year after mine. They gave me his 1959 Bell telephone phone book. It had my daddy's name written in ink at the top. They also gave me a pair of his L.L. Bean duck shoes that happen to fit me, and I've got them to this day.

They were great store managers. They were great supervisors. They were The Mavericks of Food Town Stores, Inc. They retired early. When The Mavericks left, we all sort of left together.

The retirement they got from Food Town was their foundation. Then they did what they wanted to do. We all got out from underneath the pressure. We took our jobs seriously. It wasn't that somebody was on our ass all the time. We wanted to do a good job. We wanted to do it right. We wanted to be the best in the business, which we were at the time.

At one time, we were going to acquire Lowe's Foods in North Wilkesboro, owned primarily by J.C. Faw and MDI Food Service.

They had 19 stores and we had 17. This was in 1976. We'd negotiated a price. We were gonna buy it for cash and stock. We would take over their stores and convert them to Food Towns. We would close down their offices in North Wilkesboro. They didn't have a warehouse of any consequence because they bought directly from MDI. I had my accounting boys lined up. Jim Berrier was going to go with me because it was big deal. We were going to do three stores a day 'til we got it done.

My bags were packed, I'd kissed my wife, and we got a call from the FTC about 4 p.m.

They said they were "constrained to enjoin the merger." They were going to prevent it.

We had everything on go. Ralph called Jim and me into his office and said he'd gotten the call that the FTC stopped the merger because it would constrain competition.

I said, "How will it constrain competition? They have three stores in Winston-Salem, and we have two stores in Winston-Salem that compete against them."

Now you imagine stopping a merger when you've got all the massive mergers we've had today? This was back in 1976 — President Jimmy Carter, with government coming out of every pore of your body.

So we called it all off. We spent probably nine months to a year sending them information. Finally, we agreed it was not worth the effort. We could take that time and money into building and developing our own stores and warehouses.

I was in charge of Food Town aviation. We were starting to look at locations in Florida. We weren't quite ready to buy a plane, which we did later. Joe Wilson had inherited Wilson Construction Co. from his father. They built bridges and roads and had a King Air airplane. Nice plane.

Tom Smith would ask me to line up a trip. We rented the Wilsons' plane. I worked out terms with Joe for the cost. It worked out very nicely, and the plane was there at the Rowan County airport. When Joe wasn't using it, we were able to rent it.

His pilot was a wonderful man named Lester

Beauchamp. Great pilot. He took the crew down to Florida and back. They always had hot coffee and doughnuts on board.

That's the way it was when I left. Then Food Town started purchasing their own planes.

Several years later, Lester moved out to Colorado, and was involved in a plane crash. He survived the crash, but the weather was so horrid that he died of exposure. He was flying the skiers around in Aspen. He was a neat guy. He could fly a plane through the eye of needle. But the weather got him that time.

In the early '80s, I was treasurer for Food Town Liquors, Inc. I didn't even know it. They just told me. In South Carolina, we were able to have liquor stores beside Food Town stores. I don't think it clicked, and so they sold it. I got a lot of free samples. That was nice. Being treasurer of Food Town Liquors, Inc., had its benefits.

At Christmas, we used to have a nice, three-line buffet table set up for the key people at headquarters. Also invited were store managers, the few supervisors we had, and their wives. Each year, it got bigger and bigger and bigger and eventually moved to the Crystal Lounge. We had roast beef and all the trimmings at all three lines. Ralph had a big thing about buffets and using both sides.

The party kept getting bigger. We'd give away prizes, and Ralph would talk about what we'd done that year and projections for the next year — a rah-rah type of thing.

Jim Berrier and I got a handwritten memo from Ralph one day, with an "S" at the top for suspense. His secretary would hold them for five business days — Jim sometimes answered them and sometimes didn't. I answered all of them.

It said, "We've outgrown the Crystal Lounge. Please check out how many seats are in Keppel. Let's eliminate dinner, but get first-class entertainment." He had underlined "first-class entertainment" three times.

This was 1977, and I had a little bit of devilment in me. I thought to myself, "We can have some fun with Ketner on this one."

I told Mr. Berrier, "Let me check around and see what I can come up with — 'first-class entertainment.'" I called up to New York. I forget the booking agency, but they handled first-class rock stars. I think Keppel seats 1,504 people. I said, "We're having a Christmas party for 1,500 people and we want to book a top-flight band. We'll have the introductions and we'll have music and we'll have closing remarks. Give me two of the best rock bands that would be available on this date, and the price."

The agent told me we could get Grace Slick and Jefferson Starship for $25,000 plus expenses. Or we could get the Allman Brothers band for $18,000 plus expenses. They were still hot, especially in 1977. I updated Jim Berrier on it, who thought Mr. Ketner would have a fit.

Sure enough, he got real red in the face when we showed it to him. That didn't fly. He was not thinking of THAT kinda first-class entertainment. We ended up getting somebody much more affordable. I don't even remember who now. We paid $2,000 or $3,000 — and we got a $1,000 performance.

That would have been a Christmas party people would have told their grandchildren about — the night Grace Slick and Jefferson Starship came to Keppel Auditorium for Food Town Stores Inc.'s Christmas party. And yes, I did save all my memos.

Food Town quick takes

What did that nice man say to you?

A high-level operations person was at one of our early Food Town grand openings when a little boy came into the store with his mother. The little boy would run up to the shelf and pull everything off. They'd have to call and have somebody come and fix it back up. The mother wouldn't do anything. The high-level operations man went and whispered something into his ear.

The little boy, from that point on, held his mother's hand and stood close to her skirt.

When they were checking out, the mother leaned over and asked, "Honey, what did that nice man say to you?"

"He told me if I didn't stop pulling stuff off the shelves, he'd beat the hell out of me!"

Crisco on sale for $1.98 at A&P

A female shopper came up to the manager at store No. 1 complaining that our Crisco oil costs $2.49 a bottle.

"A&P's got it for $1.98 a bottle."

Our Food Town manager said, "Well, why didn't you buy it there at A&P?"

"Oh, well, they were out."

So our manager said, "Whenever we're out of it, we sell it for $1.39 a bottle."

Does your flounder come from High Rock Lake?

I was at store No. 1 at Ketner Center doing a routine cash audit. The telephone rang, and there had just been some kind of a sewage leak from a battery factory in Davidson County that had drained down into High Rock Lake. There was a warning not to fish in the lake and eat the fish after it had been exposed to the draining.

This lady called while I was in the office. When the manager got off the phone, he was laughing.

"The lady wanted to know if we got our flounder out of High Rock Lake. I assured her we didn't get our flounder from High Rock Lake."

(Especially since flounder comes from the ocean!)

Don't approve checks from exotic dancers

When we opened our first store in Charlotte, No. 26, we were just as busy as we could be. An attractive young woman needed a check approved, and I approved it. It was for the amount of the groceries, no more, but still, I should have called for somebody else.

No sooner had she left than the assistant manager walked up and said, "She's one of the dancers over at the gas station they converted to a topless bar about six months ago."

Bound to be a high-class joint.

Sure enough, a week later, the check bounced and came back to the store. And I had some explaining to do.

A note about store numbers

Store No. 26 was actually the 16th store in the Food Town chain. There wasn't a No. 13, and the other nine stores were stores we had sold or closed before the LFPINC concept took hold.

Ralph's first desk

Food Town bought Ralph's first desk from Ketner's Supermarket. When I showed it to Glenn Ketner, Sr., he said it was Ralph's buyer's desk when he worked for him.

When we moved over to Harrison Road, we had all new furniture. They left that desk over at the warehouse on Julian Road, and they put it downstairs whenever they turned Julian Road into a refrigerated warehouse. It was a wooden desk and I knew it wouldn't last in that environment, so I bought it from the company for $100.

It's in one of the vacant houses on Parkview Circle. I showed it to Mr. Ketner once and he got a kick out of it. Everything I saved, he was so glad I saved it.

Concrete-lined filing cabinets

Jim Berrier had two filing cabinets in his office. One was his and one was Mr. Ketner's. Mr. Ketner kept financial working papers and leases for the different stores. Mr. Berrier kept petty cash and the corporate minutes book. Mr. Berrier had an extra key to Mr. Ketner's safe in case he ever needed to get in it, and Mr. Berrier had the original stock book in his cabinets.

They looked like regular filing cabinets, but they were lined with concrete and were fire-proof.

Dancing with Ruth Ketner

Whenever we went to any conference where there was a band or dancing, Ralph would not dance with Ruth. He would never say a prayer in front of a group.

Jim Berrier was a good dancer. He would dance with Ruth. As he got older, I would dance with Ruth. She enjoyed dancing and I enjoyed dancing. Once, at a conference, we danced to "Johnny B. Goode." I was 26 and I was just about dragging. She said, "C'mon, Hap, dance! Johnny's still being good!"

Ruth Ketner was another unsung hero in the success of Food Town. She was also a driving force behind Ralph's ambition and success. She was a smart woman.

Ralph Ketner's cuss jar

Toward the end of my tenure at Food Town, the Belgians, the New York bankers, and everybody kept saying, "You need to beef up your financial department. You need to get an MBA in." After awhile, Ketner bent to that pressure. So I'd have these MBAs I'd have to deal with.

I was doing what I thought was a very good job. I think history will say I did a very good job, if you look at the memos and reports. But after awhile, I got tired of the different people coming in to be MY boss, to teach ME how to run Food Town's financial and accounting departments. After awhile, I realized one of them came in and didn't do anything but take my secretary and dictate speeches for Toastmasters. That was pretty smart, wasn't it?

I didn't think I wanted to spend the rest of my life having a swinging door of MBAs and smart asses coming through. It was a fluke we became as successful as we were, they said. We were the darlings of Wall Street, but it just had to be a fluke, they said. Right? Wrong! So, I figured it was time to join the other mavericks and head on out to pasture and create a new farm.

Ralph Ketner agreed with me in the end. He said all the reasons that he eventually left Food Town were exactly what I said leaving Food Town 30 years earlier. The last time I met with him was at Catawba in the office of the Ralph W. Ketner School of Business.

The secretary could hear everything and she had a cuss jar. The last time we talked, we talked about why we left. I said the "F" word several times — surprise, surprise. The secretary out there liked me a lot. She was just a great gal. I took $20 and stuck in the cuss jar.

"You don't need to do that," she said.

"Trust me," I told her. "I used a couple of $10 words in there."

She just laughed because she had heard everything.

That's the last time I saw Ralph Ketner. Talk about closure — that was pretty neat closure.

The stages of learning

As I got older, I realized each stage of my life represented a stepping stone. What I learned in college was accounting. It was practical. It made sense to me. I also got a good exposure to liberal arts I would have never learned on my own. At the same time, it didn't make as much sense as it does now. Music, literature, art, physics. What I learned working at Towne Pharmacy was dealing with the public. At Sherrill and Smith, I learned how accounting meets the public, vis-a-vis tax returns, audits, bookkeeping, etc. At Food Town Stores, Inc., it all came together — like a hurricane! Everything was mixed in there together that I'd learned from the other stepping stones. At that point, practice totally overcame theory.

Doctrines from Mr. Ketner

• Do not lean against a desk. Stand in front of it, or sit behind it. Do not lean.

• Use a click pen instead of a twist top. You save so much time. For God's sake, don't pull a cap off and write, and then refill it with ink. I'm 68 years old, and I still have my click pen.

• When you're traveling in your car, keep the radio off. Think about where you're going, what your job is to be when you get there. Have a pad beside you, and as you think of things to do, scribble them as you drive.

• Also keep a pad and pen by your bedside. When you wake up at 2 in the morning and have a great idea, write it down. Then you can go to the bathroom and come back and sleep like a hog — not a dog or a log — because you've written it down, you can't forget and you've got something good.

• Whenever you have a woman in your office, have another woman with you, and have the door open. If you're not able to do that because of privacy issues, have a glass window into the accounting area, so everyone can see who's in and out of your office.

• No private calls. Business only, unless there's an emergency.

• If you do your job properly — it's a hobby, not a job — when you go to sleep at night you should dream about your job.

• No names on mailbox or house number to prevent kidnapping of you and your children.

Back in the '70s, there was a deal where people were kidnapping CEOs around the world for money. Ketner got upset. Ketner couldn't breathe through his nose; he had to breathe through his mouth. If someone would have taped his mouth, he would have suffocated.

We had to call in a big insurance company to analyze him for kidnapping coverage. I met with the guy for a couple of weeks and he came back to me and said, "This is a difficult task. Your boss does everything the same way. We need to get him to change his pattern of activities."

I said, "That sounds like a good idea. You go in there and talk to him about changing his activities. I won't do it."

Ralph Ketner's initial system

Ralph used various initials for typing memos:

Ralph was RWK — Ralph Wright Ketner

GEK for Glenn E. Ketner

CBK for C. Brown Ketner

WLS for Wilson Lee Smith

JJB for James J. Berrier

TOE for Thomas Olin Eller

I was HAP

Tom was TS

In the next generation, you were not granted three initials. You were only granted two.

He wrote me twice with "HR." He said, "HR stands for 'Home Run.'"

But I ended up being HAP.

Charlie Wilson was CW.

Clifford Ray was CR. I don't know why he didn't

have three initials.

Ronnie Smith was RS.

That's about all I can think of now.

Remember, the dreaded "S" at the top of all memos — the suspense file going directly to Lawanda Parchment. That meant you had five business days to answer the memo. Jim Berrier rarely replied.

A professional road map

Over the years, people have asked me why I went to Food Town to work. No matter what the financial rewards, why subject myself to that stress and pressure? The answer — I needed the experience. I needed the money, and I needed a professional roadmap for either at Food Town or somewhere else. No matter. It all worked out. I'm happy, and Food Town Stores, Inc., benefitted from my being there. All good.

An interesting footnote. I took drafting at Boyden High School and won first place in the state for drafting in 1968. In 1973 and 1974, I drafted the design for phase 1 of our headquarters on Harrison Road and submitted to architect Robert Stone. He liked them, and drew formal certified plans, which became a 13,000-square-foot structure built by

Hendrix and Corriher in Mocksville. A year later, I drafted Phase 3, a 14,000-square-foot structure. Mr. Stone and his team approved it. Construction began. My first plans drawn for phase 1 called for 15,000 square feet. Ralph cut them back to 13,000 square feet. No explanation. Just do it!

What if?

More times than I care to admit, I wake up in the middle of the night and wonder, what if? With the team of Mavericks inherited from Glenn Ketner, Sr.'s organization, what if the corporate climate had been one of nourishing and positive reinforcement instead of the whipping post mentality? I can't help but think what could have been. Ralph Ketner developed a winning strategy from that grocer in Ohio. Ralph's LFPINC could have changed retailing nationwide, not just groceries. These thoughts have haunted me for years. What if?

I'm happy with the way my ventures and my life have turned out. And I'm most thankful to Mr. Ketner and Food Town.

But I still wonder, what if? Damn those dreams in the middle of the night.

What if?

All good things must come to an end

When I first joined Food Town I figured I would spend my entire working life there. Over the years it became clear this would not happen. As much as I loved the company and The Mavericks, it just didn't seem to be a lifelong venture.

Longevity and nurturing were unfortunately not part of the culture. How many people older, maybe wiser, had been in my shoes before I was? Now they were long gone. I did my best. I made the company money — a lot of money. And I certainly learned from it all and was rewarded handsomely for my efforts.

Had I stayed at Food Town, who knows? Looking back, I think I came at the right time. I left at the right time. The company was good to me. I was good to the company.

The lessons and experience learned from The Mavericks? Invaluable!

Maybe at best I could have gone a few years more, but Ralph hired a little fellow who had convinced him he could be the financial captain that could take the company to the next level. Wow! Really?

I came into my office one morning and there were more than two dozen vitamin bottles on my desk.

The little fellow came in and told me how each worked. Oh my. I told him I would take a look at them.

"Jolly good!" he yelled.

Who do I need to f*** to get out of this movie?

The next day, I went out to my assistant and asked what the overnight CD rates were on our excess cash. She said the new little fellow was having her type a speech for a club he was in. She said she would get to it as soon as she was finished.

Soon after, I caught the flu going around. I was depressed. Was it time to go?

Going into business for myself

I took a year off. I had not gotten my CPA certification because Ketner told me I didn't need it to work at Food Town. I'd been out of college 10 years, so I went back and took some review courses, and studied. I spent time with Annette. Heather was just at the right age I could spend some time with her. I enjoyed doing things I couldn't do before. Heather went to North Hills through fifth grade. I'd take her to school and pick her up. On Saturdays, we'd go out to a nice place to eat and see a movie together. Sometimes, on Sunday after church, Annette, Heather and I would go to Charlotte and go to lunch and see a movie as a family. Once I took Heather to see "Nightmare on Elm Street." I didn't know it was gonna be that damn scary. We walked out and she said, "Dad! You shouldn't have taken me to see that."

I loved that year. I took the CPA exam that summer 1982 and passed the two hardest parts. That fall, I took the other two parts and passed them. I started an accounting firm, H.K. Roberts. Paul Hinkle, a Salisbury attorney and CPA, joined me as partner.

Moving to Pine Tree Road

Uncle Wilbur Roberts built the house at 21 Pine Tree Road in 1946, and I bought it in October 1978 at the ripe old age of 27, not long before my birthday. Mr. Leo Campbell was the contractor, and I'd always admired it. I played over there as a child with my cousin, Jean. Her brother, Stanley, was off to military school, but Jean was always there. I spent a couple of nights there when my dad was in the hospital. Uncle Wilbur also had a nice house at Blowing Rock. It was two-story stone house with a beautiful view of the mountains. He was in the cotton business with Daddy and Papa.

My Aunt Thyra wanted to downsize and we were wanting to buy a larger house. Heather was 11 months old, so we sold our home in Westcliffe and bought hers. When we were in our 30s, we had plans to add on to it in the back. But we never did. We did add on a bathroom off our bedroom and an extra closet for me. Now it's the perfect house. As you get older, smaller is better.

Ralph Ketner bought the house across the street from us. He and I moved into the neighborhood about the same week. Then, Ralph went through a separation and divorce from his wife, Ruth, so Archie Rufty bought it.

Archie had been living behind us on Confederate Avenue. He gave that house to his daughter and moved in across the street from us. Archie was an attorney and had been a judge. He was a practicing attorney when we moved in. Archie told me Uncle Wilbur got him into the stock market. Archie went on to become a legendary investor. He was a later investor in Food Town. Archie and his family moved out to Las Vegas sometime in the late '80s, and I never saw him again. But he was always a good friend of the Roberts family.

Ryan's Steakhouses

In 1984, I got interested in a young company called Ryan's Family Steakhouses. Archie Rufty was completely head over heels for this company.

I said, "Archie, it's just a steakhouse."

"Yeah, but they do it the right way."

So I started researching Ryan's. I talked to Charlie Way, who was vice president and corporate controller. He and I got to be friends over the phone. Then Annette, Heather and I stopped in Greenville, S.C., on a trip to Sea Island, Ga. We met the founder, Alvin McCall, Charlie Way, and corporate secretary Janet Gleitz. We all liked one another, and I decided to start buying Ryan's stock.

About five months later, they asked me if I'd go onto the board of directors. I said no, because I was getting my second wind from getting out of the corporate world. They asked again three years later. I went on the board then, and served 18 years on the board of Ryan's Family Steakhouse. At one time, we were part of the S&P 500. It was a great company. It helped fill a hole in my soul of not being in a big, corporate environment like Food Town had become. A part of me missed that. Going on the board of Ryan's was just enough to fill that need.

A hedge fund eventually approached us about buying Ryan's. I went on the vetting and discovery committee of this company, and also opened it up to other hedge funds that might be interested in buying, to level the playing field. After about six months, we came to terms and sold it, and all resigned from the board that day. We sold the stock at near an all-time high.

A job well done.

That officially ended my ties to big business. I settled into life in the slower lane at Statewide Title, Inc., and have loved it ever since.

I loved my years at Ryan's and I loved my years at Food Town. But that's why we have seasons. These were my corporate seasons: Food Town, Ryan's, the CPA firm, Statewide.

Back in the groove

The CPA firm was a lot of fun. It got me back in the professional groove. My health was good, and has continued to be ever since by not having such a fast-tempo pace.

On March 1, 1984, I founded Statewide Title. The original name was First Title of Salisbury, Inc., because we didn't plan to go out of the county. A couple of years later, we expanded and changed our name to Statewide Title, Inc. It's grown to serve all 100 counties in North Carolina.

Statewide issues title insurance through three major, national underwriters: First American Title, Chicago Title, and Old Republic Title. Title insurance insures the title to property, which companies and individuals purchase after their attorneys have done a title search. We deal directly with the attorneys, and we insure their title searches.

Statewide works with 600 attorneys across the state. I'm in North Carolina in every county twice a year, just checking in with clients. Our in-house counsel is Chris Burti. He's been with us close to 23 years. He knows more of the N.C. general statutes that relate to real estate than anyone else I know of in our state. Yet he's not an egghead. He's a neat guy. He has a sailboat and loves sailing with his wife, Linda Carol. Chris lives in Farmville and works daily with his right-hand person, Diane Hobgood. She backs up our office and we back up theirs.

We were the first title company in North Carolina to execute a title insurance transaction online. I made the decision early on to invest in viable technology. You can spend millions of dollars on technology that isn't worth a damn.

I made a list of the 20 worst employees I've ever had. I tried to glean out of that what I don't want in an employee. There is one imperfection in an employee that I cannot successfully deal with or tolerate, and that is a bad attitude. I'm on my toes when they first come in wanting to know what the company can do for them, not what they can do for the company.

I like it when employees have worked in high school or college, not spoon-fed by their parents. A good work ethic is a must, along with a willingness to learn. I want down-to-earth folks, coming from down-to-earth families, with an ability and eagerness to learn.

Statewide has 12 employees here in Salisbury and two in Farmville. Excluding one new hire, the years of service range from 8 to 35 years. We pay well. We have good benefits, and we operate the company like a family in a safe environment. Tell me how you can beat that combination. Statewide has had its challenges over the years, but with our great team now assembled, we look eagerly to the future and to many more years of growing the company.

Origins of Statewide Title
By Annette Roberts

In 1983, when Hap and I began talking about opening a second business, Sted Morris, a good friend and stockbroker in Durham, called to see if Hap might be interested in purchasing some title insurance stock. We were just learning about title insurance. Hap began studying title insurance, which was relatively new on the scene in North Carolina. He bought some title insurance stock to receive annual reports. He decided to research the possibilities of opening a small agency in Rowan County.

Sted offered a wealth of information. He grew up in Salisbury but had his practice in Durham. He was quite successful and thought a lot of Hap from his days at Food Town and Ryan's Family Steakhouses, and they had stayed in touch. After studying title insurance, Hap realized that North Carolina had the lowest premiums in the nation and margins would be extremely tight, but he decided to give it a try as he was accustomed to dealing with slim margins in the grocery business. After much preparation, Hap opened First Title of Salisbury.

Hap was still practicing accounting with the accounting firm of Hinkle and Roberts, CPAs. As both companies grew, Hap realized he had to make a choice between the two. He joined the title company — which had opened about two years earlier. Hap's robust personality, sense of fun, and keen intellect made him quite an asset to the title company.

Jeanette Lassiter, Paul Hinkle and Darrell Whitaker continued to work with both companies. When Hap joined First Title full-time he asked if I would like to be involved in the company. I will never forget that day. I was so happy to be asked as my teaching career had become disappointing. But since Heather, our daughter, was only about 6 or 7, I declined and said that I would love to be more involved in a few years. Hap had a sharp team member in Jeanette Lassiter, who worked well with attorneys. Jeanette was quick to learn anything she put her mind to, including title insurance. She was and continues to be an invaluable asset to Statewide's growth. My interest was in marketing. Several years later, I joined the company full-time in marketing and loved it!

Title insurance is one of the most competitive businesses in the state. We were experiencing an economic slow down when I joined Statewide Title. We needed someone in marketing full-time, and we could not pay much — so that role had my name on it. I did not cover the entire state as we had a state marketing manager. I marketed to Rowan County attorneys and clients, and to the real estate attorneys in counties adjacent to Rowan, and boy, did I love it. It was hard work, but I thoroughly enjoyed helping grow the company. We pulled through the slowdown with the dedication of our fine staff and increased marketing.

As First Title grew to include all counties in the state, we changed our name to Statewide Title Inc., and the rest is history. Title insurance has been good to the Statewide family. We are appreciative of our Rowan attorneys along with all of our real estate attorneys and clients throughout the state. In 2019, Statewide Title observed its 35th anniversary. Because of its early leaders' hard work and their skilled mentoring of the second generation, we have survived and grown over the years. Statewide is a blessing to us all.

A few words from longtime Statewide employees

Hap and Annette and I have seen our children go to school together. We've supported each other through the deaths of family members. We've shared a lot of laughter and a lot of tears — but that's life. I can't imagine myself anywhere else. Life is good. Life is real good.
Jeanette Lassiter, vice president and state manager

Hap has always taken the high road, without exception. You don't have to prod him to do the right thing. The longer Hap gnaws on the bone, the more he's gonna come up with stuff — and you realize he's not gonna run out of bone.
Chris Burti, senior legal counsel

Hap has always taken care of his people. They do the family business thing right. You don't feel like an outsider. This company is its own entity. That's what Hap and Annette have made it. I will begin my new role at the end of 2020. But this is Hap

and Annette's business, and we will continue to follow their plan as long as they choose.
Chris Preslar, vice president and director of development; and president-elect of Statewide Title (slated to begin December 2020)

It has been a pleasure to work for Hap and Annette at Statewide Title, Inc. I'm thankful they've given me the opportunity to work here with them. I look forward to many more good years together to help grow Statewide Title. God always provides.
Wanda Peffer, corporate controller and treasurer

Hap and Annette have watched me grow up here, and they've been a part of every aspect of my life. They are truly family.
Kellie Martin, operations manager

I started working at Statewide when I was a college student. In doing business, Hap likes to take a proven model and find ways to improve on it. He and Annette keep things interesting, and the variety is what's kept me here.
Steve Jacobs, IT/special projects

Hap has given me more than a job, more than a salary, more than a friendship. He has given me the freedom to live out my calling.
Charles Church, property manager

The Statewide campus

The building that houses my office was my Aunt Mabel Roberts Hoffner's house. Annette and I bought my parents' house when they passed away. The Krispy Kreme property was where my grandfather lived. That was sold in the 1960s. If I'd had the chance, I would have gotten that property. We've got right much property right here. We bought the surrounding houses going down Merritt Avenue to Greg Scarborough's house on Parkview Circle to store old files. These houses insulate the campus here. Annette and I also have my parents' four-unit apartment house that is now offices. There are offices downstairs and two apartments upstairs.

My man cave is here. I've got an area where we have oyster roasts and shrimp boils. At one time, it was a seven-car garage. I've got a home theater in there, so some of my buddies come over after church and we can watch Westerns. Or if the Panthers are winning — which they haven't been lately — we get pizza and watch the games. And the German Shepherds come in and they sit and watch with us. My first Shepherd, I bought for my girlfriend at Catawba and I kept it in my apartment. My girlfriend went home for Christmas and never came back. That was my first German shepherd. I've had them off and on ever since. I've had black Labs in between, and, of course, hunting dogs.

The dancer and the panic attack

One year, I told the paralegals we worked with that if we attained a certain level of business per week, Statewide would host a Hawaiian luau around the pool at Country Club of Salisbury. I would dance with several hula dancers as part of the festivities.

We met the goal.

I'd just gotten back from Jamaica on a fishing trip with Annette and my hair was pretty long. I had it put in cornrows. I wore a Panama hat with flowers in it, a coconut bra, and a grass skirt with swim trunks underneath. I was to be the back-up dancer to the professional dancer. Another local actress with Piedmont Players Theatre said she'd dance with us. We went to the dance studio and practiced.

The evening of the party came. They cleared the pool at 5 p.m. as our people started arriving in festive dress. There were about 100 women there. I was in the women's dressing room to practice with the two dancers one last time. We were getting ready to go out and the girl came up to me and said, "I can't do it. I'm having a panic attack."

I said, "I'll take the lead. Just line up behind me and I'll do the best I can."

We did it, it worked, and everybody hooted and

hollered. Everybody had a great time. It was a big success.

As a footnote, when Joe Taylor managed Belk, they'd have a fashion show at Keppel Auditorium at Catawba College. Keppel holds 1,504 people. That same dancer asked me if I'd dance the tango with her at the fashion show. I kindly and respectfully declined. I could just see her having a panic attack in front of 1,504 people.

And speaking of dancing, longtime friend Sandy Lee says that Hap's dance card is always full.

"I will never forget Hap's 50th birthday luncheon at the Country Club of Salisbury," she says. "All the guests were women. He is such a character and we never know what he might do next!"

Keep on dancing, Hap.

Mr. Ketner takes us to lunch

Mr. Ketner took the whole Salisbury office to D.J.'s one day and treated us all for lunch. When we were leaving he said, "Hap, I'm mighty proud of you for what you've done here, building up your business. One day I'll be looking down at you, smiling." I'd waited a lot of years to hear those words.

One of the last times we played cards, I said, "Mr. Ketner…."

He looked at me with that cold look I hadn't seen since the working days at Food Town.

He said, "Are you mad at me?"

I tensed up, out of habit. When I went to work for Food Town, the only people who used "Mr." were Ralph Ketner and Wilson Smith. Everyone else used their first names.

I said, "No, Mr. Ketner, I'm not."

He said, "Why don't you call me Ralph?"

I said, "Habits are heard to break."

He said, "Why don't you start calling me Ralph?"

So I did.

Stewart Morris, Sr.

One of my buddies called me recently. Stewart Morris, Sr. Great guy. He just wanted to talk. Stewart is in his mid 90s and is dating a sweet, smart lady. Stewart taught me much about the title business. We liked each other from day one.

His late wife's father wrote the articles of secession for the State of Texas as Texas entered the Confederacy. He has a French-built private jet. Once on a trip with him to his sailing yacht "The Petty Cash," in Tampa we almost crashed with a FedEx plane. Wow! Stewart's pilots were right, and FedEx was wrong. But a good outcome!

The Heimlich maneuver

In 2015, we took the Farmville office out to lunch. That evening was prime rib night at the Hilton, so we decided to have dinner there. It was packed. I was sitting behind a woman and all of a sudden, her husband stood up and said, "Somebody, help! My wife is choking!"

Everyone was yelling, "Call the manager!"

I turned around and lifted her up and did that jerk one time. Nothing happened. I did it again, and a glob of prime rib came out. Both she and her husband told me I'd saved her life. They asked for my business card, but I never heard another word about it.

Ironically, I'd never been trained in the Heimlich maneuver.

The Roadhouse

The Roadhouse started out when my parents bought their property in 1940 from the City of Salisbury. You couldn't buy one lot; you had to buy two. They bought two lots for $400, total. They built their little house on the one lot, which is now 115 N. Merritt Ave. Daddy went up pretty close to the end of the second lot and had a little barn built, a little stall for his mule. He planted a big garden with his plow and his mule.

In 1950, they decided to build a four-unit apartment house there and Daddy no longer had his mule on the property because he'd bought his big farm four years earlier. They built around that little stall and made a five-car garage, four units for the four people who rented the apartment and the fifth unit for Mother to park her car. His garage with his car, shovels, and tools, is now gone.

About 15 years ago, we started having oyster roasts and barbecues for clients and set up in the garage. About 10 years ago, I had two more garages added to store cars in. We got to where we'd put serving lines in there during oyster roasts or shrimperoos.

Back in my Ryan's Family Steakhouse days, I thought the name Happo's Roadhouse would make a good restaurant name. I always knew that name would see the light of day.

So about 18 months ago, I got the idea of enclosing the five-car garage. We put in three heat pumps and put in lighting and did an overall fix-up so that I could have guys over year-round. That would be my man cave, so to speak. We put big screen TVs in there. We could still do oyster roasts and shrimperoos, because we could raise the four garage doors and put up a tent with shucking stations and seating.

I've got a fourth phase I'd like to add on, 20 feet by 20 feet, that would have restrooms and a full kitchen with ice maker. I've got the preliminary plans and the engineering work. I've got to pull the trigger but I'm not ready yet. I've got other projects going and I don't want to spread myself too thin. That property is not going anywhere. We've got bathrooms, we've got kitchens, so we're OK.

Sometimes, after church, I'll have 10 or 12 guys over to watch a Western. Kent Roberts will fix hot dogs and pop popcorn, or I'll go out and get pizzas. We just sit there like little boys, watching movies and having a big time.

If the Panthers are playing out of town, sometimes we go in phase 3 where the big screen TV and club chairs are and watch the game. Kent Roberts will fix popcorn and we have soft drinks.

It's turned out to be a pretty neat thing. I'll go down there when I need to work and go into phase 1 and take Lilli, my little dog. Charles will bring the two German Shepherds in and I'll let them chew on a bone. I'll turn on music low or the TV low and go through stacks of work.

I don't want to bring the big dogs up there to my office. They're too big. I had a pair of antique Oriental ginger jars underneath the portrait downstairs of Annette, Heather and me. One of the dogs was in such a hurry to get up the steps that her tail hit one of the jars and broke it. I was going to give the other one to Heather for Christmas but I dropped it and it broke into a thousand pieces. I hustled out to Lillian's Library and got her another antique ginger jar.

Hence, no big dogs coming up here. They can go into the Roadhouse with Daddy.

Pack rat

I'm a pack rat and it's in my genes.

For example, I'll like something like baseball cards I collected as a kid, and then be on to something else. It boils down to what interests me. I'm a man of various interests, and, as I said in the preface, I'm a complex man. If I get interested in something, I try to immerse myself in it. I've amassed enough knowledge to talk about a variety of different subjects.

I've got time now, too, to get away from some of the day-to-day stuff at work, and study up on things that interest me. How or why do I stop? Fortunately, I get bored with stuff. I'm not gung-ho about any one thing. I'll go on to something else. I don't always have to be conquering new frontiers.

I probably will hit my saturation point when I go to my mausoleum.

My idea of hell would be having to do the same thing over and over without some type of variation.

For example, auditing at Sherrill and Smith. That just drove me crazy, ticking off every fifth entry, going to the file cabinet and checking against discrepancies. When I had my CPA practice, I realized I didn't want to be a practicing CPA because I didn't have the patience for it.

Statewide Title was closely akin to Food Town Stores, Inc., and Ryan's Family Steakhouse, so that was my cup of tea. We started Statewide from scratch, from the ground up — nothing our forefathers had done, but something that we built ourselves.

When we started, the title insurance business in North Carolina was pretty much in its infancy. Then banks started requiring title insurance. We got in and carved out our piece of the pie and developed our niche. That's my definition of an entrepreneur, identifying and developing a niche.

It took me about a year to formulate what could be the next step after the CPA practice, but for a while, be connected with the CPA firm. Jeanette Lassiter worked in accounting and Statewide Title. I did, too. For several years, we wore two hats, sometimes three or four until I finally sold my share of the practice to Gary Morgan. I thought there was more potential in Statewide Title than there was in a CPA firm — more room for growth, more room for expansion, more room for everything.

My family

Annette and I met on a blind date in 1973. She was a senior at Appalachian and I had just graduated from Catawba and was working my first year at Food Town. We were introduced by one of my best friends, Kee Kirchin. We hit it off from the beginning. We had both dated different people in college. Just about every concert I went to with a date in Charlotte, she went to see the same bands at Appalachian with her dates.

Annette had a vibrant personality, was so attractive, and was lots of fun. For me, she "checked all the boxes." She grew up on a dairy farm and was not only a hard worker but good with her money. She believed in saving and has saved part of almost every paycheck she has ever received.

We got married April 27, 1974. Heather was born Oct. 29, 1977. I was an only child, so we were happy with one child. Heather's been a wonderful daughter, and she has a great personality. She lives here in Salisbury and is married to Brad Brady. They have two children, Bell Elizabeth, born Jan. 15, 2010, and Graham Roberts, born April 14, 2015. He was born early, but he sailed through it. He's a ball of energy now.

Heather works here Tuesday-Thursday as a marketing representative and assists in the office. She is a valued player. She has a business degree with an accounting emphasis from Salem College. I encouraged her to major in business. I thought it would be good for her to have that background. Heather was a bright child. She started reading early, and all the feedback we got told us she was pretty sharp. She's a well-rounded individual.

Over the years, we have always celebrated our birthdays together. I'm Oct. 24 and she's Oct. 29. We took her to New York for her birthday on several occasions. On this particular occasion, we stayed in a suite at the Waldorf-Astoria Hotel. We went to the 21 Club for dinner. We ordered steaks, and Heather said, "Daddy, this is a good steak, but I like them at Ivan's better!"

As a family, we mainly traveled to the beach and mountains. During my time of building up my CPA firm, Annette and I bought a lot in Piney Creek, N.C., overlooking the New River. We got a contractor who was working for Cannon Mills. On the weekends, he and I would go up there and work. We loved that place. You could see three states. Many times, I'd call Annette at 3 and say, "Pack up Heather and the dog, and let's go up to the mountains for the weekend."

We kept the place for about five years, and then Heather got busy with church youth group and spending time with friends. But it was fun when she was younger and just the three of us would go up there. We'd go to Shatley Springs to eat, and we'd go canoeing on the New River.

We now have an oceanfront townhouse at Wrightsville Beach, which was damaged in Hurricane Florence. We had to wait awhile to get it fixed, because there was more damage there than there were contractors. Typically, we go down and spend two weeks at a time, maybe four or five weeks a year. Heather and her family go, too, at other times. Annette and I both have offices there and we both call on attorneys there, so we earn our keep.

We have a farm, called The Triple R, on Bell Farm Road in Statesville, right across the street from Annette's family farm. Half of it has 40 head of Black Angus cattle — owned by Annette's brother, Burt Bell — and the other half we lease to her cousin, Rex Bell, who has grain.

The Sigmon family owned the land. We bought four different adjoining tracts in 2007, 2008 and 2009. It has a nice, spring-fed branch that we might put a pond on sometime. We fenced in three different pastures — One, Two, and Three, is what we call them — and Burt has his cows there.

Heather was on the equestrian team at Salem and has always had a love of horses, which she has passed on to Bell. Bell talks in terms of "when she owns the farm," she will have "an arena here and a barn there, and a tack room there." She's got it all figured out. Not sure how Annette and I will fit into her plans.

Bell and I go out on the Gator and she'll say, "Poppy, can we go a little faster?" I say, "Bell, when we are doing this, I'm looking in the woods to make sure there's no trash. You don't just need to be out here on a ride, you need to be surveying your property."

And then we'll go around and survey all three pastures to check the fence lines. Burt is good about checking it, but Bell and I like to do it ourselves, too. I am instilling in her a stewardship of the property.

Bell takes horseback riding lessons from Stacey Carter, just like Heather did. Stacey teaches riders everything from A-Z, including cleaning out the stables and all of the non-glamorous aspects of horseback riding.

Annette Bell Roberts
About Annette

Annette was born to L.P. Bell, Jr. and the late Joyce Barker Bell on May 19, 1951, the first of four children.

"I was the bossy one," she admits.

She was educated in the Iredell County Schools. She graduated with honors from Appalachian State University in 1973 with a degree in English, and she was a member of the English Honors Program. She received a master's degree in education from UNC-Charlotte and taught school for several years.

Annette and Hap met when Annette and her

roommate, Hilda Upchurch, came to Salisbury to student teach. Kee Kirchin and Kee's girlfriend, Joyce Boyette from Wilson, introduced them in 1973. But they never thought the relationship would work — especially Joyce.

"When I first met Hap, I thought he was cute as a button, a go-getter, and charming," Annette says. "He was such fun and his keen sense of humor still ranks among his best qualities. Never a dull moment with Hap."

"God had other plans"
From Kee and Joyce Kirchin

Kee and Joyce Kirchin met at Appalachian in September 1970. He was a junior from Salisbury and she was a freshman from Wilson. They married in 1974 after she graduated.

What made them think Hap and Annette would be a good match?

"That's an interesting question," Joyce says. "I didn't think it would work out whatsoever."

"Hap needed a date," Kee adds. "Everyone else we'd come up with didn't work."

"Hap was too much of a rogue," Joyce says. "Annette seemed so sweet and gentle. She'd grown up in the country — and then there was Hap."

"We weren't matchmakers by any means," Kee says, "but God had other plans."

After six weeks with Hap, Annette knew she was in love.

Kee adds, "Hap is an acquired taste, but he's probably my first friend along with Locke Long, Jr. In all the times I've been with Hap in these crazy situations at college or the beach, there was never anyone who didn't like Hap. Hap is one-of-a kind, a true original.

"He was also a capitalist from the get-go. He was going to be successful. He was a great draftsman. I am a retired engineer, and Locke is an engineer, and we both thought Hap would be an engineer, too, but he got into other things."

The Cookie story

Right before I met Annette, I was dating a girl from New York, and her name was Catherine. I was just crazy about her, and I went out to Belk to buy her a Christmas present. If you bought three silk scarves you got them monogrammed for free. So I bought three with C monogrammed on them. We went to Thanksgiving holiday and she hooked up with a boy she knew in high school and never came back to Catawba. A couple of weeks later, Kee and Joyce introduced me to Annette.

Belk called and said I had to come get the scarves. I said I did not want them.

I thought that whole night about what I was gonna do with them. I didn't know what the hell to do. I'd spent $20 plus tax. It hit me about 5 o'clock in the morning: When she came home from school for the Christmas holidays, I started calling her "Cookie."

People called her Cookie for years.

"Joyce and Kee had Hap pegged after all," Annette says. "He was and is a mess, but I have really enjoyed the nickname 'Cookie.'"

Heather Roberts Brady
From Heather

What's it like to be Hap's daughter? It's fun! My personality is kind of the opposite of my parents. I'm probably more of a natural introvert, to be honest. As a child, I learned to roll with it. It's really been good for me to have such extroverted parents. Growing up, it was always fun. Sometimes I got embarrassed, but we were always laughing.

From my childhood, I remember Dad always being the cool dad. The words "cool" and "fun" are what stand out in my mind. And he was always very loving and supportive. Mom was always the bad cop. Totally. But he was every once and a while. When I was 18, I was at Salem College and got a speeding ticket. My buddies and I were going to Boone for the weekend. We were going down 421 at the North Wilkesboro Speedway, and it was something really crazy — like 40 miles over the speed limit. I had never had a ticket.

After the weekend was over, I called Dad. I was like, "You cannot tell Mom. I do not know what to do. Tell me what to do."

He was like, "This is between us. You cannot breathe a word of it and I will not breathe a word of it."

He said he'd call an attorney in Wilkesboro. He said it was Russ Ferree, the same attorney for Junior Johnson. Mr. Ferree got me off on a PFJC. I didn't have to go to court. It was years until Mom found out. He didn't lecture or anything, but he did say, "Don't do this again."

I think he was worried about Mom finding out.

Dad got me a worker's permit for Statewide when I was 14. It was important to both of them that

I started work early. One of the first summers I remember being here, Meredith Lassiter Brincefield, one of Jeanette's daughters, and I hauled files from one building to another. We moved files from basements in wheelbarrows. Wheelbarrow after wheelbarrow full of files. We had to weed out pages of this stinky old paper. We had several lists of what to throw away and what not to. Meredith and I are good buddies, so we had fun together. I was here every summer until college, and I did a little something different each year.

At Salem, I majored in business with a concentration in accounting because I enjoyed that in high school. After graduation, I moved to the beach for several years and worked in Statewide Title's Wilmington office.

I moved back to Salisbury around the fall of 2007. I walked into a mess because the economy was so bad. We had a lot of layoffs. It was an interesting time, but it was also a happy time in my life because that's when my husband, Brad, and I started dating. When I was in high school, he was my tennis instructor. He's four years older. We got married on April 11, 2009, and we have two children, Bell, 9, and Graham, 4.

Growing up, one of my fondest memories of Dad — something he has totally passed on to me — is his love of music. He would come up to my room, because I had the best stereo, and play air guitar. He was just so into it. He'd take me to concerts when I got old enough: Tom Petty, Lollapalooza, Ringo Starr. Those were some really fun memories with just me and my dad.

We listened to "Eminence Front" by The Who, and until I was 20, I thought the lyrics were "Lemon in his butt."

Mom and Dad would dance in the driveway a lot when my friends would come over. I was a little embarrassed but I kinda thought it was cool. There was always music on and they liked to show off. They are good dancers. I like to dance, but I'm not as good as they are. I have many fond memories of my parents as I was growing up.

In particular, Christmas Eve was a time for me and Dad. We went to McAdenville a lot on Christmas Eve while Mom played Santa Claus at home. Those are some really fond memories. When I got a little bit older, we'd go out to parties, and that was fun to get dressed up with him. We'd go over to Clyde's, go to Tripp and Katherine Murdoch Clement's and see old friends, go to Gerry Wood's. We would party hop. As I said before, it was fun to be with him, because he walks in and he's the life of the party. It's great fun being the daughter of Hap Roberts.

Sam's, cigarettes, and the credit card

I used to have a fellow who served as my assistant. Heather was a senior at Salem College and on the equestrian team. She stayed in a neat, older dorm with three suitemates. One day, my assistant and I went to Sam's in my pick-up truck and loaded it full of stuff to take to the girls at the dorm. Except for the cigarettes. Heather bought Salem Lights by the carton.

("Busted," Heather says.)

We loaded it full of water and other supplies, you know, stuff you need in a dorm room. My assistant started hauling it into the dorm, and the girls were tickled to get all that stuff. All of them came in and thanked me. I started telling the group some stories about my college days, and we all had a good laugh.

I went horseback riding with a date once. The horse panicked and went crazy and, of course, I was very upset. Just in the nick of time, the Walmart manager came out and unplugged it. And that date never went out with me any more.

Heather was sort of embarrassed I'd come over and brought all this stuff — and told that groaner of a joke. One of the girls put on a Prince album, and the suitemate and I danced to "Raspberry Beret." Then we tipped our berets and slipped on out.

I had to sign for Heather's first credit card. The bill came in and it was more than $5,000. I thought it was mine so I signed off on it and sent it to Wanda and she paid it.

"The best day of my life!" Heather says. "I wasn't really thinking. It just got away from me, but the bill was eventually addressed."

A therapeutic relationship

When I left Food Town, I was totally worn down. Heather and I started spending a lot of time together. She was 5 then, and was very much a daddy's girl.

I'd take her to school every day and pick her up. We would fix lunch together and listen to a lot of music together. In the mornings before school, we'd watch "3-2-1 Contact," "Mister Rogers' Neighborhood," and "Electric Company." Annette left to teach school about 7:30. We'd lie on the sofa to watch our programs, until we had to leave for school at 8.

One morning I fell asleep and Heather didn't wake me up. I heard the cartoons and knew I'd overslept.

We got into the Fabulous Z-Car and took off for North Hills.

Our relationship was therapeutic for me, and helped me regain my strength, composure, self-confidence — all things that had been drained out of me at Food Town. That was just the nature of the beast.

We weren't that close until then because I was gone all the time.

We put in a little bed upstairs where Annette's office is now and a TV on the wall. I kept office hours and studied for the CPA exam. After school, Heather could lie down and watch TV or take a nap until we went home in the afternoons. I looked after Heather in the morning until we went home for our afternoon programs until Annette came home.

She pulled me out of the dumps. I was on a trash heap.

"That was the time we were building our relationship," Heather says, "and that means a lot to me to hear about it now."

Heather and the beach

One summer we let Heather go to the beach and work. We could have pushed the "no" button but we didn't. We helped her move in and we were horrified at the slum she moved into. They loved it and thought it was the greatest thing in the world.

One of the three other girls dated a big guy. So the guy goes in and sits on the commode and the wood was rotted out and he goes through the floor into the first-floor apartment. The landlord came over and chewed the guy out — you don't just plop down, he told him, you ease down. That was the end of the summer so they made it OK.

I've always been proud to be a part of my entire family — on both sides. But over the years, it's been really cool to be related to my Uncle Ralph, and to be a part of the legacy he shared with one of the most beautiful women in the world.

Part III: Uncle Ralph and Marilyn Monroe

Undated photo of Ralph Roberts.

The uncle everybody wanted to have

My Uncle Ralph was the uncle everybody wanted to have. He gave me his WWII medals when I was about 5, and I have them to this day. He would come to Salisbury three or four times a year from New York. He was on television shows during the 1950s such as "Your Show of Shows." He wanted to be an actor. He studied under several prominent acting coaches. He met Marilyn Monroe in Lee Strasberg's kitchen at the Dakota Apartments. I couldn't wait for him to come to Salisbury for visits. He was fascinating, and he liked me. He liked to think of me as his younger brother. As I got older, we'd talk on the phone about more adult things. I never asked him questions about Marilyn. I would just sit there with a beer and see if he talked. Sometimes he did, sometimes he didn't, but I never pushed that.

He was a pack rat, sort of like I am. I was the beneficiary of his estate and settled everything. We bought a plot over near our mausoleum at City Memorial Park. First, we bought 11 plots over there on a hill, looking toward here, where my office is. I was in my mid-30s, and I knew artisans who made mausoleums were dying off. So I got with Salisbury Marble & Granite and looked at what they had. We chose a four-unit mausoleum. It has 27,500 pounds of white Georgia marble, and we paid $38,000 for it back in those days.

I like to plan ahead.

I didn't care about being cremated and I didn't care about being buried. That left the mausoleum. I've even had it power washed once. Uncle Ralph has a headstone made of white Georgia marble. My dad was buried at Rowan Memorial Park, and I didn't care about him being that far out. So when my mother passed away, I had him moved to where she was buried. I got them a nice, white Georgia marble headstone. Ralph Ketner is buried down the hill from our plots. Even in death, he was fortunate. Damned if he didn't get buried next to one of the prettiest women in town. Even in death, he is hitting grand slams.

In order to supplement his income, Uncle Ralph decided to become a masseur. He was fully licensed in Swedish massage. He kept a list of clients, and he never agreed to massage anyone unless he felt he could develop a relationship and rapport with them.

In addition to Marilyn, his clients included: Carol and Walter Matthau, Ruth and Milton Berle, Jennifer Jones, Mary and Arthur Schwartz, Jayne Mansfield, (he also choreographed the massage in her "Will Success Spoil Rock Hunter?"), Nancy Malone, Paul Burke, Shirley Jones, Marcy and

William Shatner, Fran and Perry Lafferty, France
Nuyen, Norma Crane, Maggie McNamara, Paula
and Lee Strasberg, Anna Strasberg, Julie Harris,
Geraldine Brooks, Maureen Stapleton, Jan
Miner, Judy Holliday, Betty Comden and Steve
Kyle, Phyllis Newman and Adolph Green, Joan
Lorring, Allyn McLerie, George Gaynes, Robert
Lewis, Margaret Leighton, Joan Plowright, Milton
Goldman, Arnold Weisberger, Felicia and Leonard
Bernstein, Lauren Bacall, Zoe Caldwell and
Robert Whitehead, Burr Tillstrom, Alan Shayne,
Sono Osato, Arthur Laurents, Eva LeGallienne,
Ellen Burstyn, Imogene Coca, Arturo Toscanini,
Gloria and James Jones, Betty Field, Gloria
Vanderbilt, Herbert Berghof, Montgomery Clift,
William Redfield, Gloria Safier, Helen Hayes,
Richard Burton, Jo Sullivan Loesser, Sally Ann
Howes, Richard Adler, Marc Blitzstein, Paul
Davis, Nancy Berg, Martin Ritt, Evelyn and
Richard Avedon, Leigh Taylor-Young, Joan and
George Axelrod, Shirley Clurman, Nancy Cardoza,
Philip Anglim, Diane Ladd, Dolly Fox, Kay
Norton, David Merrick, Susan Strasberg, and
Natalie Wood.

He traded acting lessons with Lee Strasberg for
massages. They all had their own cereal bowls to
have breakfast there on Sunday mornings — an
open invitation to be there for breakfast. James
Dean was there in the earlier years. Marlon
Brando and Julie Harris were there, too. One

Sunday morning in 1957, Ralph said to someone, "Who is that good-looking woman over there?" They said, "Are you serious? That's Marilyn Monroe."

Marilyn had a high IQ. Ralph had the second-highest IQ of anyone tested at Fort Jackson, S.C., when he was drafted. So they hit it off. One night, Ralph was massaging Marilyn, and she said, "Do you ever read any Willa Cather novels?" He told her he was just thinking about a novel he'd read by her. They just became kindred spirits — extremely smart kindred spirits.

Once, Marilyn was staying in a bungalow at the Beverly Hills Hotel, and called Ralph about 2 in the morning. "Please come over and give me a massage." Ralph was walking down the dark sidewalk, and he heard a voice that startled him, saying, "Your hours are about as crazy as mine." It turned out the guy was a bodyguard for Howard Hughes. They talked a bit, then Ralph went on to Marilyn's bungalow and gave her a massage.

Marilyn was part Irish and had a smooth complexion. She loved to be massaged with Nivea lotion. She would sip on a Magnum of champagne during her massages. Marilyn did not like and could not drink hard liquor. One time, Ralph picked her up and she was flustered. He didn't ask any questions.

She said, "Rafe, do you have any alcohol in the car?" (She always used the British pronunciation of his name.) He said, "You know I do. Look in the glove compartment." There was a pint of vodka, and she just took a swig of it and put it back. He didn't ask what was wrong and she didn't offer an explanation. She was upset.

Ralph thought Marilyn died of an accidental overdose of prescription medicine and champagne. She'd built up a high tolerance. She'd called him several times before when she thought she'd crossed that line. He'd break into her apartment and get her up and walk her around. The day she died, she and Ralph were going to have dinner together. She'd just bought a bungalow in Brentwood and was proud of it. She'd always rented.

Their favorite thing to do when they grilled out was fix mimosas, and Ralph would have vodka and tonic. They would charcoal steaks, toss a salad, and have baked potatoes. They'd sit around and talk about books they'd read. Ralph would give her a massage and then slip on home.

The day of her death, Aug. 5, 1962, they were to do that exact schedule. Ralph called several times during the day and couldn't get Marilyn to the phone. Ralph viewed it suspiciously but didn't push the matter, so he went ahead and made other plans — regrettably.

Regrettably because he got the last call Marilyn ever made. His answering service received a call from a groggy woman asking for Ralph.

When Ralph got the news she had died, he just went out and started walking. I said, "Why were you walking?" He said, "I went out walking and walking and walking. It saved my life."

Marilyn got him an invitation to JFK's birthday party where she sang "Happy Birthday" to President Kennedy. But Ralph and a couple of other people rode around town, listening to it on the radio.

Having the connection to Marilyn is part exciting, part curse, part happiness, part sadness. The end, of course, was a tragedy. She was a kind person.

As I said, Ralph was a pack rat. When Ralph and Marilyn and Marilyn's half-sister went up to Roxbury, Connecticut, to get what Marilyn wanted out of the farmhouse she and Arthur Miller shared, she went over to a closet and found a coat.

When Uncle Ralph died, my cousin Claudette Roberts and I went to his house. We thought we would try to clean it up. I suggested the first thing we do would be to go through his clothes and take them to Goodwill. He wanted things like that to be used by people who needed them.

There were two fatal mistakes I made in cleaning out that house. This is one of them. There was a lady's Burberry trench coat in a closet. I wondered whose it could be. I said, "Well, a friend of Ralph's just left it over here, and he saved it. Try it on and see if it fits."

"It doesn't fit me," Claudette said.

"Put it on the truck," I said.

Flash back to Marilyn, Ralph and Marilyn's half-sister at the farmhouse. Marilyn took the coat out, a Burberry trench coat, paused, walked over to a trashcan and threw it away. Ralph said, "Marilyn, that's a good coat, it can do somebody some good." She said, "You want it, you take it," and walked out of the room. It had the scent of another woman's perfume on it.

A month later, we found a list of Marilyn's things Ralph had, and on it was a Burberry trench coat. I thought that's where the story ended.

Charles Casillo is an author, actor, and playwright. I told him that story about giving it to Goodwill. He said, "You know the rest of the story, don't you?" I said, "No, I don't."

He's the one who told me about giving the coat to Ralph and smelling the scent of another woman on it. I didn't know that until about six months ago.

My second fatal mistake was that I found a cigar box full of hotel keys. These were old keys that had the actual key and a wooden tag on it with the name of the hotel on it. I threw those away. There again, when I found the list, there was a list of hotels Marilyn stayed in, and Ralph had the spare keys.

I pretty much kept the rest of the stuff: manuscripts, pictures, letters, 3x5 index cards of her lines, "A kiss is nice, but a diamond tiara is much nicer."

I've been approached about donating the collection to UCLA, the Motion Picture Academy of Arts and Sciences, the University of Southern California, and other places. All of these items are securely stored off campus.

Casillo told me there are hours of tapes of Ralph being interviewed at UCLA. If Annette and I ever go back to California, I'll go. I've heard most of it from the horse's mouth — straight from Ralph. He spent the last three years of his life in Salisbury. Annette and I went to New York every December to visit him. We always met in the Oak Room of the Plaza Hotel. We would have drinks and talk.

Sometimes we'd go at Thanksgiving and have brunch at the Plaza. Other times we went and stayed at the Waldorf Astoria and had brunch there.

In 1957, my mother, father and I took the train to New York. We were seeing Ralph in a play and he was going to take us around town. My dad had some business there, too. We stayed at the Roosevelt Hotel. Ralph had his 1957 black Corvette with red leather interior that I was just in love with.

And so, on a Sunday afternoon right after lunch, Ralph picked us up. Daddy sat in the passenger seat and I sat on his knee. He had a pillow for the hump so Mama could sit there. It was a gorgeous, sunny day in New York.

He took us down to the East Side where Imogene Coca had an apartment overlooking the East River, and we went up and visited. She had plush white carpet throughout her apartment. She had two Standard Poodles, one black, one white. She was quiet, not like most actors you see on TV. I played with the dogs and Ralph and Imogene and Mom and Daddy talked for an hour. I enjoyed that and that was all well and good, but across town was Marilyn Monroe.

Years later, I asked him why he took us to see Imogene Coca. He said, "I thought you'd like playing with the dogs."

I thought to myself, "The dogs?!! I wanted to meet Marilyn."

I could have been a charming kid. Marilyn loved charming children.

Once in the 1950s, one of Imogene's husbands or boyfriends got drunk and out of order, and she called Ralph over. The guy started giving Ralph a bunch of shit. Ralph told me later, "I don't know what made me do it, but I hauled off and hit him in the face. It dazed him, so I put him in a closet and locked it. Then he started yelling."

Then he made a veiled threat to Ralph, "I'm gonna tell Dorothy Kilgallen."

She was a longtime panelist on "What's My Line?" and a syndicated columnist who wrote "The Voice of Broadway." That threat didn't matter to Uncle Ralph. He laughed about it.

Annette and I went to New York a year to the day before John Lennon was shot. Ralph came over and picked us up. We drove around some, and he took us over to the Dakota. We went up on the elevator to Lee Strasberg's apartment. Lee's second wife and their small children came to the door and let us in. He'd just finished making

"Godfather Part II." The apartment had high ceilings, heavy tile floors, and bookcases everywhere with movie posters of different stars.

Lee was meeting with Al Pacino, who we also enjoyed meeting. Lee Strasberg had inherited Marilyn's white baby grand piano. We chatted with Lee and Al and then left, and Ralph stayed.

Preface to "Mimosa," an unfinished manuscript
By Ralph Roberts

So many truths, half-truths, speculations, out and out fabrications, and, especially, phantasmagoricals have been written through the years about Marilyn Monroe, that I think the time has come for me to finally put down on paper the Marilyn I got to know, love and respect during the three and a half richest years of my life.

I have read very little of the many books, articles, and exposés published about Marilyn since Aug. 5, 1962 [the day Monroe died]. Enough has filtered from excerpts to make me realize that most have very little in common with the person I knew. In fact, I would not have spent ten minutes with the one so portrayed, much less the hours, days, weeks, months and years that I did.

I told my decision to write about Marilyn to Lee Strasberg. "Wonderful, Ralph, wonderful! You're the one who could furnish an overall portrait of her. She told me quite often that you were the one person in the world she felt she could tell anything to, that you were the brother she always wanted. It'll be difficult to relive much of these years, but I'm delighted that you will try to set the record straight on the rare and beautiful person that she was."

I have spoken to hundreds of people through the years since Aug. 5, 1962. Each has his idea of Marilyn, good or bad, but never indifferent. Everything in the world has been written and said about her. Even outside of the world — where Marilyn really was. She was everything special to everybody. She was one of the originals. A UFO.

When I finally decided that I should write my memories of Marilyn Monroe, I took two drinks of vodka and water, made a toast to her; there seemed to be a tangible expression of approval…

I have admired much of Norman Mailer's writings. I met with him when he was writing his book. Read the galleys. Suggested several incidents that did not jibe with what I knew…

All of this leads me to the reason for finally writing these memories of Marilyn. I knew her. She was an innocent. I suspect I am an innocent. We had a curious closeness from the beginning. Probably from childhood associations. I was born with a physical condition as I was "tongue tied." She was a stutterer in her youth. She once remarked to me on this: "God has a way. Each of us starts out with the good and the bad. Sometimes the bad turns out to be the best thing that could have happened. It makes you try harder."

I did know her. Loved her. What I am writing about is the Marilyn I knew. Not hearsay. Not from interviewing people who knew, or wished to have known her. Not from reading material written about her through the years. Not from seeing her movies. As a matter of fact, I have seen very few of them. But from knowing her. From reconstructing incidents from my appointment books, from scribblings. From tapes I spoke into on every occasion I could manage. These, I found early on, were for me, an easier way of keeping my diary than writing…

When I determined, for better or worse, to write about Marilyn, I think the decision was made, subconsciously, by this theory. If I were to write down, even if for myself, chronologically and in as much detail as possible, that period of time, maybe, as in "The Bridge of San Luis Rey," it would become clear about the shadows. Why we were all gathered for that moment on Aug. 5, 1962.

Set the record straight. Goethe said, "If you call a bad thing bad, you do little; if you call a good thing good, you do much." Most of what has been written about Marilyn Monroe seems to be an interest in portraying her badly ... There's a prevalent belief that calling anything bad, bad or good, is gold in the bank.

Marilyn's death

In August 1962, my dad met me at the entrance of the old First Presbyterian Church. We were joining Mama to go in to the service. Daddy said, "Marilyn Monroe died last night." I was 10 years old, and I was stunned. I asked, "How is Uncle Ralph?" Daddy said he was upset.

Later that day, Uncle Ralph called Daddy and said he was devastated. He said he and Marilyn were to have cookout supper at her new bungalow in Brentwood last night. Uncle Ralph called three times that day but was told she was not available. Very odd. But Uncle Ralph, unfortunately, made other plans.

Late that night, he got a call on his answering service that most experts consider to be Marilyn. She was in trouble, uncomfortable with her meds and champagne. Ralph had received this call before, and always went to her aid. But this time he was not there. The last call. The telephone in her hand when she was found. Marilyn had lost her life. And Ralph his best friend.

Not knowing what to do he began walking. He walked for hours until he couldn't walk anymore. Roberts family members don't cry, but he cried and he cried and he cried.

A young girl who stuttered and a young boy who was tongue tied now were separated. Gorgeous people. And now Marilyn dead. I could not believe it. The world could not believe it. Marilyn Monroe was dead at 36.

A bad day

When my Uncle Ralph died, it was also a bad day. He had come back to Salisbury to live. He would come over to the office every day. We would have a beer or cup of coffee and he'd put the dogs up. Back then they were black Labs. He died April 30, 1999.

He didn't come over that day. We were sitting downstairs in this building. Jeanette Lassiter and a co-worker went over to his house and they said his papers are still out in the yard. We all went back over there. They told me not to go in the house. He had died during the night of a heart attack. We called Dr. Bill Thompson and he came over.

It was real hard on me and I was having a tough time dealing with that. He was the uncle everybody wanted to have. He lived in New York City, and would send me this and send me that. I ended up with a lot of his things.

Bill Thompson suggested I go see Barbara Lowry about grief counseling. She's a great gal and super professional. Then I started talking to her more and more about business. She said she could have released me years ago, but she's been a wealth of comfort over the years.

Biography in Internet Movie Database (IMDb)

Hap Roberts was born in Salisbury, North Carolina, on October 24, 1950, the son of Harold Knox Roberts, Sr., a cotton broker, and Idell McNeill Roberts, a school teacher. Roberts married the love of his life, Annette Bell Roberts, in 1974. They have one daughter, Heather Roberts Brady. Hap graduated from Catawba College in 1972 with a degree in accounting. Upon graduation, Mr. Roberts was employed as an accountant by Sherrill and Smith, Certified Public Accountants. In August 1972, he left there to work for Food Town Stores, Inc., now Food Lion, Inc. and retired as its Corporate Controller in 1982. In 1983 he opened his own accountancy practice, H.K. Roberts, C.P.A., later to become Roberts and Morgan,

CPA's. This firm now exists as Gary D. Morgan, CPA. In 1984, he opened a title insurance agency, Statewide Title, Inc. of which he is president and co-owner with his wife, Annette Bell Roberts, vice president. This company provides title insurance protection for property owners throughout North Carolina. Mr. Roberts' uncle, Ralph L. Roberts, was masseur, close friend and confidant to Marilyn Monroe. Ralph impressed his love of acting and film upon Hap, who is now a devotee of both. Hap continues to support the arts and to preserve their history for the appreciation of future generations.

Various book acknowledgments

"The gregarious Hap Roberts, nephew of one of Marilyn's greatest friends, Ralph Roberts, added another level of understanding to that multifaceted friendship."
Charles Casillo, author of "Marilyn Monroe: The Private Life of a Public Icon."

"My thanks go to fellow Marilyn biographers who have given me support on this project … I thank Hap Roberts of Salisbury, North Carolina, for giving me access to 'Mimosa,' Ralph Roberts's unpublished memoir, as well as other Roberts papers."
Lois Banner, author of "Marilyn: The Passion and the Paradox."

Uncle Ralph and James Dean

Ralph had an apartment in Greenwich Village in the early '50s, a great hangout for artists, aspiring actors, and neat people. It was not unlike Paris in the '20s. This talented group came from all over, and studied under New York's brightest: Lee Strasberg.

Ralph and James Dean and Julie Harris became friends. They would go to Ralph's apartment along with others and listen to the latest tunes on Ralph's phonograph. So many members of this group had so much talent — too much to end, too soon for one. Ironically, General Joseph Stilwell whom Ralph served under in Burma, died much too soon. East and West — Stilwell with the Eastern influence and Marilyn with the Western. Sometimes the two do meet.

The Willa Cather connection

The first time Ralph massaged Marilyn was around midnight in front of a roaring fire. Ralph was thinking about a Willa Cather novel he'd read earlier that day. Suddenly, breaking the quiet, Marilyn asked Ralph, "Do you ever read Willa Cather novels?" Ralph was stunned. That was the beginning of the chemistry between two kindred spirits — two very complex people.

The two were not unlike Willa Cather. She was born in 1873 in Gore, Va., and was a novelist who wrote about frontier life. Marilyn and Ralph had all her writings. I have Ralph's Willa Cather novels now. I have some of Marilyn's.

Occasionally, I gingerly take one off the shelf and begin reading, and I feel like Ralph and Marilyn are with me.

Marilyn and Salisbury

Mark Wineka wrote about Marilyn's connection to Salisbury in a 2012 feature about Marilyn and Ralph Roberts.

"Roberts became Monroe's official masseur in 1959, and for long periods, during her various marriages and romantic entanglements, would give her massages daily.

"Roberts and Monroe forged a bond. She called him 'Rafe,' the British pronunciation for his name.

"They connected on the Willa Cather books they read, their spirituality and, believe it or not, Salisbury.

"As Roberts massaged her at night, he spoke to her about his hometown and all of its places and people — down to men such as Irvin Oestreicher and Julian Robertson Sr. to the roasted peanuts at the Lash store and the winged statue on West Innes Street."

The making of "The Misfits"

During the making of "The Misfits" — Clark Gable's final film role and Marilyn's last complete role — there was a lot of tension on the set. There was friction between Marilyn and Arthur Miller. At one point, Gable told Ralph they would not have completed the movie had Ralph not assisted Marilyn through his frequent massage sessions and steadfast attention to her.

All was not tense. One afternoon, Marilyn and Ralph were driving down the hills from Reno when a small Fiat zoomed by them. They were shocked at the speed and recklessness of the driver of the Fiat. Ralph told Marilyn, "This isn't going to end well."

Sure enough, a few minutes later they came upon the Fiat. It had rolled over and was spinning. Ralph and Marilyn waited for the Fiat to stop spinning — not knowing what to expect much less do when it did. Finally, it stopped. An irritated man extracted himself from the driver's seat, kicked the overturned Fiat, and hurled the insult "asshole" to the battered vehicle.

Ralph and Marilyn, laughing after they realized the driver was unharmed, proceeded on their merry way.

"The Misfits," Mom and Me

When the day finally came in 1961 that "The Misfits" came to Salisbury and played at the Center Theater (where The Meroney is now), Mom and I went to an afternoon matinee.

I loved the movie, but my mom did not care much for it. There was a lot of drinking and lot of implied sexuality. When Marilyn ran up on the beach and flopped down beside Clark Gable, Mom stood up and said, "We've seen enough."

I swear I think I grabbed her by the leg and she dragged me up the aisle. I wanted to stay, but she had enough. Seeing Marilyn Monroe, a grown woman, I didn't know why, but I really liked it. Sort of like the first time I had some cantaloupe when I was 3 or 4. I don't know why, but nobody had to tell me it was good.

A couple of years later, I finally saw it at the drive-in. I just thought it was wonderful, and I liked everything about it.

When Uncle Ralph was in Reno, I got his mailing address from my dad, and sat down and wrote him a letter. I asked him if he could get me an autographed picture of Marilyn Monroe, and if possible, to get her to sign an autographed picture to my girlfriend, Kay Snider.

About four weeks later, I got a call from Kay, who was excited. She said she had gotten a manila envelope in and it had a picture, autographed, "To Kay from Marilyn Monroe." Then I got a manila envelope with an autograph, "To Hap from Marilyn Monroe." It was on the cover of Life magazine in which Marilyn was on the front with Yves Montand, and I have it to this day.

Sadly, Kay passed away several years ago. Before she died, we talked at length several times, and I once asked if she still had her autographed picture.

"Unfortunately," she said, "Mama threw it away when I went to college."

Damn the bad luck!

Norman Mailer

Norman Mailer wrote one of the first credible books after Marilyn died. He did an extensive job of interviewing people, including Uncle Ralph. In 1963, Playboy interviewed Mailer, primarily about his book. My dad bought a couple of copies of the magazine from Towne Pharmacy and was sitting in the den reading the interview.

"Daddy, what are you reading?" I asked.

"There's an interview this month with Norman Mailer, and he's written an extensive book on Marilyn, and Uncle Ralph is in it quite a bit," he said.

So, I asked my father if I could read the interview.

He said, "It's fine with me. Just check with your mother."

I checked with Mama, who said, "Just read the interview and you don't need to get into the jokes and everything else."

Now, I'm a slow reader.

Every day for a week, my mom asked if I had finished the interview. I said, "I'm getting there, I'm just a little slow."

In the meantime, I'd memorized every playmate and pin-up that was in that magazine.

Finally, Mom said, "Time's up, let me have the magazine."

Architectural Digest

Marilyn bought her bungalow in Brentwood and began fixing it up. Uncle Ralph said she had never been happier. That's why it's so hard to understand why the coroner concluded she had committed suicide.

In 1994, Architectural Digest featured Marilyn's former home in its April issue, called "Hollywood at Home." The entire issue featured nearly three dozen stars at home, headlined by Marilyn in the article, "Marilyn Monroe: The Nomadic Life of a Screen Legend." At the time of her death, she'd just purchased a 2,300-square foot Spanish-style hacienda at 12305 Fifth Helena Drive in the Brentwood section of Los Angeles.

Toward the end of the 10-page piece, the writer Donald Spoto quoted Ralph Roberts in this excerpt:

In early 1962, Marilyn planned a partial renovation of the house and went to Mexico to buy furniture. In Cuernavaca, Toluca, Taxco and Acapulco, she shopped for native furnishings, cushions and tapestries and looked for Mexican tiles to install in her new kitchen and baths. "Marilyn was very happy," recalled her friend Ralph Roberts. "She was really taking control of her life and asserting herself." All those close to her agreed.

Most of her purchases were still undelivered when she died, and so her dream of a place of her own was never fulfilled. But her desire to leave a legacy was — in twenty-nine films. She still stands for something funnily unsolemn about sex, something truthful and vulnerable.

When Norma Jean turned into Marilyn Monroe

One day, Marilyn and Uncle Ralph were walking down the sidewalk in New York City. No one recognized her. All of a sudden, Marilyn turned to Uncle Ralph and said, "Do you want to see it?" Meaning, the transformation from Norma Jean Baker into Marilyn Monroe. Her demeanor changed, people started recognizing her, and she and Uncle Ralph ended up having to run to their destination.

Flight insurance

Uncle Ralph said that before every flight Marilyn ever took, she always bought flight insurance. That way, she reasoned, the plane wouldn't crash.

The 50th anniversary of Marilyn's death

I was asked to speak at the 50th anniversary of Marilyn Monroe's death but declined. I don't know why — I just didn't feel right about it. I had a conflict here in town, which I could have gotten out of. It was in LA. I just didn't do it. Maybe I'll attend the 60th anniversary event if invited.

Elvis and Marilyn

Uncle Ralph visited Marilyn's final resting place at least twice. On both occasions, he saw Elvis Presley there. Several years before, he'd met Elvis at a party, and Elvis remembered him. They exchanged pleasantries.

Marilyn Monroe's funeral

Only 31 people were invited to Marilyn's funeral. They included:
- Berniece Miracle — half-sister
- Joe DiMaggio and Joe DiMaggio Jr. — ex-husband and his son
- Lee and Paula Strasberg — acting coaches
- Dr. Ralph Greenson and family — psychiatrist
- Allan Snyder — make-up artist and close friend
- Inez and Pat Melson — business manager
- Sydney Guilaroff — hairdresser and friend
- Agnes Flanagan — hairdresser
- Anne and Mary Karger — longtime friends
- George Solotaire — friend of DiMaggio and Marilyn
- Pat Newcomb — publicist
- Eunice Murray — housekeeper
- Rudy Kautzky — chauffeur
- Florence Thomas — maid
- Enid and Sam Knebelkamp — one of Marilyn's foster parents
- Aaron Frosch — attorney
- Milton Rudin — attorney
- May Reis — secretary
- Ralph Roberts — masseur and close friend
- Erwin and Anne Goddard — Grace Goddard's family

The never-ending question: Hap's answer

How did Marilyn die? Was she killed? Was it a conspiracy? Was it suicide? My answer — based on more than 50 years of questions and listening to Ralph — is this: By an accidental overdose of alcohol and prescription pills — not mixed together for death — but mixed together for a good night's sleep to combat her never-ceasing insomnia. It was an easy albeit a dangerous practice.

This theory isn't sensational. It doesn't sell books. This theory makes people's eyes glaze over. I'm sorry, but that is my answer to this question, and I firmly believe it.

Rest in peace, Marilyn.

Part IV: Our final thoughts

Life with Hap

Life with Hap has been a trip. Hap is so full of fun, so full of dreams, and so full of himself. He is truly hard to keep up with sometimes.

From day one, Hap made me part of everything. Being married to Hap is like going to college all the time. He has so many interests and becomes absorbed in learning everything that he can about these subjects and of course, his excitement pulls me in, too. He is a collector of everything and when the UPS driver stops at Statewide, we all know that most of the boxes are for Hap.

Hap and I are like two peas in a pod. We enjoy the same things, enjoy working together on the Statewide campus, and especially enjoy being in different buildings. We love our work and have to work hard to cut work off when we come home. We love Statewide and we love our Statewide family.

We have been through ups and downs, some very serious, as with Hap's surgery so many years ago. This was so hard on him. He was very sick. Over the course of a year, he lost lots of weight and was so weak. He never complained once. Later when Hap did leave Food Town for health reasons, he used that period to spend quality time with Heather and to study for his CPA license. It was time well spent on both. We have a wonderful daughter, and the fact that Hap is a CPA has been a plus for Statewide.

Hap always makes lemonade out of lemons. He always gets things done. He is always positive. His mother was the most positive person I have ever been around besides Hap. That great positive attitude continues and it rubs off on all around him. When he was so sick during the Food Town days and was in and out of the hospital, he kept "The Power of Positive Thinking" by Dr. Norman Vincent Peale nearby. He still has it in our bedroom right along with his Bible.

The things that brought Hap through the difficult time of his surgery and afterward were his positive attitude and his determination to get well and move on and start new exciting work ventures. Heather and I were totally supportive in every step of his recovery and remain so today.

Hap and I are soul mates and have had a ball all through our 45 years of marriage. We've had so many happy times and so many blessings from God. Being with Hap has definitely been a trip but the ride has been exciting and the trip continues.

Annette Roberts
November 2019

Epilogue

Throughout this book, I've been meditating on the three major parts of my life, which we included in the title: my life on North Merritt Avenue, my time at Food Town, and my responsibility in carrying on my family's role in the legacy of Marilyn Monroe.

When I was a child, my whole universe centered on North Merritt Avenue. In many ways, it still does. We have the Statewide Title campus here, and Annette and I spend most of our days here. Right now, we don't want to be anywhere else, although we are training a group of capable folks to step up when we decide to take a smaller role. While physically debilitating because of my ulcerative colitis, my time at Food Town was instructive to me in a way that no other company could have been. When I left Food Town, I had the tools, wherewithal, and determination to strike out on my own, and I did just that, forming my own CPA firm and later, Statewide Title. Our work with Statewide is literally that — we work with attorneys and clients all over the state of North Carolina. Our reach expands beyond North Merritt Avenue.

Finally, after being entrusted with all of Uncle Ralph's papers and memorabilia regarding Marilyn Monroe, I take seriously the role of being the keeper of his legacy as it is linked with that of

Marilyn's. In doing so, we are sharing Marilyn's story with the whole world, and we want to be as balanced and accurate as possible.

Just as ripples flowed out from a splash in the old neighborhood pond all those years ago, the memories of my life have flowed out of me. I hope you have enjoyed reading about some of those memories, and I hope to continue to relish those memories for many years to come.

Hap Roberts
November 2019

Index

Adams, Allyn...........108
Agner, Chris...........44, 46, 60, 85, 86
Agner, Martha...........85, 86
Atwell, Tom...........26, 27
Banner, Lois...........220
Barker, Angie...........81, 103
Barringer, Bill and Mabel...........58
Basinger, Dick...........38
Basinger, Mabel...........37
Basinger, Mike...........35, 36, 38
Basinger, Ode...........35, 36, 37, 38
Batista, Fulgencio...........80
Beauchamp, Lester...........151, 152
Bell, Burt...........191, 192
Bell, Joyce Barker...........8, 122, 192
Bell, L.P. Jr...........8, 122, 192
Bell, Rex...........191
Berra, Yogi...........32
Berrier, Jim......116, 128, 129, 130, 131, 132, 140, 145, 146, 147, 148, 150, 153, 154, 158, 159, 164, 165
Bouknight, Mr. and Mrs...........59
Bost, Vick...........43
Brady, Bell...........122, 124, 125, 189, 191, 192, 197
Brady, Brad...........122, 124, 125, 189, 197
Brady, Graham...........124, 125, 189, 197
Brady, Heather Roberts..........8, 43, 107, 112, 117, 118, 119, 120, 121, 122, 124, 125, 138, 168, 169, 171, 176, 186, 189, 190, 191, 192, 195, 196, 197, 198, 199, 200, 201, 202, 219, 234, 235
Brando, Marlon...........206

Brincefield, Meredith Lassiter 117, 197
Brockman, Max..73, 74, 75
Burti, Chris..173, 177
Burti, Linda Carol..173
Butler, Charlie..48, 49
Campbell, Leo...169
Carter, Jimmy...151
Carter, Stacey...192
Casey, O.L...131
Casillo, Charles.......................................210, 211, 220
Castro, Fidel...80
Cather, Willa..207, 221, 222
Cauble, Gary...140
Chandler, Bob...78
Chene, Miss..81, 82
Choate, Walter..149
Church, Charles.......................................50, 178, 186
Clement, Tripp and Katherine Murdoch..................198
Clyde..198
Cochran, Ethlene...24
Coca, Imogene..206, 212, 213
Cook, Elizabeth..9
Crockett, Jim..59
Dean, James..206, 221
Detty, Wendell..92
DiMaggio, Joe...104, 230
Dorton, Leighanne...43
Driscoll, Betty..60, 61
Eagle, Vera Roberts...22
Eddleman, Wayne..40
Edwards, Barry..113
Edwin...52, 53, 54, 55
Eller, Tommy....................116, 131, 140, 146, 147, 164
Ellis, Ann..114

239

Eure, Thad..24, 75
Faison, Buck..78
Faw, J.C..150
Ferguson, "Big Hon" and Mrs..........................32
Ferguson, Robert "Knee High"..........26, 27, 30, 31, 32, 33, 45, 46, 56, 80
Ferree, Russ..196
Frazier, Dr..149
Freedman, Michael......................................60, 61
Gable, Clark..223, 224
Garner, Keith..87, 89
Gleitz, Janet..171
Glover, F.O..27, 149
Goethe..217
Hale, Rip..58, 59
Hall, Trina..95
Hardister, Jay..56, 57, 72
Harris, Julie..206, 221
Heffner, Oren..142
Helms, Jayne..114
Hill, Barry..9
Hinkle, Paul..169, 175
Hinson, Mr...38
Hobgood, Diane...173
Hoey, Clyde..75
Hoffner, Mabel Roberts 22, 23, 50, 131, 179
Hughes, Howard..207
Hurley, Jimmy and Gordon...............................64
Ingle, Norman..56
Jackson, Reggie..106, 137
Jacobs, Steve..9, 123, 178
Jimmy..52, 53, 54, 55
Johnson, Junior...196
Kay, John..95

Kennedy, John..209
Ketner, Brown................................131, 146, 164
Ketner Sr., Glenn......128, 131, 146, 148, 158, 164, 166
Ketner, Linda..82
Ketner, Ralph........9, 12, 82, 98, 123, 128, 129, 130,
    131, 132, 133, 134, 135, 136, 140, 141, 143
    144, 146, 147, 150, 152, 153, 154, 158, 159,
    160, 161, 162, 163, 164, 166, 167, 168, 170,
    181, 182, 205
Ketner, Ruth..159, 170
Kilgallen, Dorothy...213
King, O.W. "Fred"...24
King, Sheila Pfeiffer..24
Kirchin, Aileen..84
Kirchin, Joyce Boyette 9, 193, 195
Kirchin, Kee..............9, 14, 51, 52, 83, 84, 85, 188, 193,
    194, 195
Landers, Ann..84
Lassiter, Jeanette...............9, 50, 58, 175, 176, 177, 188,
    197, 218
Lee, Sandy..9, 181
Lennon, John..213
Long, Jean..55, 68
Long, John..69, 70, 71
Long, Jr., Locke..........9, 14, 42, 44, 50, 55, 56, 60, 64,
    65, 67, 68, 69, 70, 71, 83, 90, 92, 101, 194
Long, Sr., Locke...........................64, 65, 70, 71, 78, 79
Long, Ruby..55
Lowry, Barbara...219
Lyerly, Mildred...81
Mailer, Norman..215, 226
Mantle Mickey..32
Marsh, Bill..149
Marsh, Donnie.......................................116, 131, 149

Marsh, Ronnie..............................116, 131, 149
Martin, Billy...137
Martin, Kellie...178
Mays, Willie..46
McCall, Alvin...........................113, 114, 115, 171
McCutcheon, Dr. 81
McNeill, Bob..14, 24
McNeill, Ida Covington....................20, 23, 30, 41
McNeill, John Alexander..............................20, 23
McNeill, John Charles "Hap"......19, 20, 22, 23, 28, 99, 100
McNeill, Lura...24, 30
McNeill, Nell...14
Medlin, Fred..93
Mesimer, Grace..60
Michalec, Sarah....................................2, 9, 123
Miller, Arthur..209, 223
Monroe, Marilyn..................104, 105, 203, 204, 205, 207, 208, 209, 210, 211, 212, 213, 214, 215, 216, 217, 218, 220, 221, 222, 223, 224, 225, 226, 227, 228, 229, 230, 231, 236, 237
Montand, Yves...225
Moon, Keith..94
Morris, Sted..174, 175
Morris, Sr., Stewart................................182, 183
Musselman, Bill.....................................39, 149
Morgan, Gary........................140, 141, 188, 220
Murphy, Lynch...91
Myers, Edna Roberts 22
Oestreicher, Irvin...222
Pacino, Al..214
Parnell, Ann Roberts..........................back cover
Parchment, Lawanda...................................165
Parrott, Dida..9

Peale, Norman Vincent..235
Peffer, Wanda..9, 50, 123, 178
Petty, Tom...198
Pfeiffer, Grace McNeill..24
Poe, Andrew...13
Poole, Lee Buck 35, 36, 37
Preslar, Chris.....................................9, 123, 177, 178
Preslar, Dewey...140
Presley, Elvis...229
Ragan, Brad..87
Raley, Larry...108
Ray, Clifford.....116, 129, 131, 140, 143, 146, 147, 164
Raynor, George "Voodoo"............................46, 47, 48
Raynor, Jimmy "Doo-Doo"...... front cover, 44, 45, 46, 47, 102
Reeves, George..32, 33
Roberts, Annette Bell..........8, 107, 109, 114, 115, 119, 121, 122, 123, 124, 125, 126, 132, 138, 143, 144, 150, 168, 171, 174, 175, 176, 177, 178, 179, 180, 186, 188, 189, 190, 191, 192, 193, 194, 195, 196, 198, 200, 201, 211, 213, 219, 220, 234, 235, 236
Roberts, Bonnie Idell McNeill.......8, 20, 21, 23, 24, 28, 30, 31, 33, 36, 39, 40, 46, 54, 55, 66, 74, 80, 84, 90, 106, 118, 184, 205, 212, 217, 219, 224, 226, 227, 235
Roberts, Carl West.............................22, 24, 25, 26
Roberts, Claude Murray "Dimp"..............................22
Roberts, Claudette..209, 210
Roberts, Clyde..22
Roberts, Sr., Harold K.......8, 19, 20, 21, 22, 24, 25, 26, 27, 28, 29, 30, 31, 32, 33, 34, 35, 36, 37, 38, 39, 40, 41, 45, 47, 48, 54, 55, 56, 60, 73, 74, 75, 76, 77, 79, 80, 90, 101, 102, 106, 149, 169, 184,

205, 212, 217, 219, 224, 226
Roberts, Hugh Kerr.........19, 21, 22, 27, 28, 29, 40, 75, 80, 169, 179
Roberts, Jean 169
Roberts, Kent.......22, 44, 45, 46, 48, 49, 68, 69, 87, 88, 89, 185
Roberts, Lula Clementine Walker.............................21
Roberts, Ralph...8, 22, 104, 105, 106, 118, 202, 203, 204, 205, 206, 207, 208, 209, 210, 211, 212, 213, 214, 215, 216, 217, 218, 219, 220, 221, 222, 223, 224, 225, 226, 227, 228, 229, 230, 231, 236
Roberts, Stanley...169
Roberts, Thyra..169
Roberts, Walter Lee "Brud"..22
Roberts, Wilbur Franklin.....19, 21, 22, 29, 52, 80, 169, 170
Robertson Sr., Julian...223
Robinson, Edward G..52
Roosevelt, Franklin..22
Rufty, Archie 49, 170
Rufty, Ed...48, 49
Sambo...49
Scarborough, Greg..179
Sherrill, Bill...78, 128, 134
Shinn, Cora..9, 13
Shinn, Ed..13
Shoemaker, James...113
Slick, Grace..154
Smith, Mike...72
Smith, Ronnie.......................................116, 148, 165
Smith, Ted..28
Smith, Tom...9, 132, 133, 151, 164
Smith, Wilson.........116, 130, 131, 140, 146, 147, 148,

164, 182
Snider, Kay...225
Spoto, Donald..227
Starnes, Bob and Lillie...37
Starr, Ringo...198
Stilwell, Joseph...22, 221
Stone, Robert...165, 166
Strasberg, Lee...........204, 206, 213, 214, 215, 221, 230
Tate, Jack..113
Taylor, Beau..116, 131
Taylor, Gary..136
Taylor, Joe..181
Thomas, Bob and Arva..59
Thomas, Karen...59
Thompson, Bill...19, 218, 219
Tomes, Kimberly, Miss USA 1977..............................108
Troxler, Bud and Red..39
Turner, Jim...13
Turner, Susan Shinn.....................................12, 13, 123
Upchurch, Hilda..193
Walser, Marianna Long..55, 68
Ward, "Big Bill"..59
Way, Charlie..113, 171
Wenig, Mike...9
Whisenant, Chris...86, 87, 88, 89
Whisenant, David...88
Whitaker, Darrell..175
Wilson, Duane..140
Wilson, Charlie...164
Wilson, Joe...151
Wineka, Mark.......................................9, 133, 138, 142, 222
Wood, Gerry...198